CREATIVE COLOR

2016 Fair Isle

Collection

BY KNIT PICKS

Photography by Amy Cave

Printed in the United States of America

Second Printing, 2016

ISBN 978-1-62767-130-9

Versa Press, Inc
800-447-7829

www.versapress.com

CONTENTS

INTRODUCTION

Named after a tiny island in the north of Scotland, Fair Isle knitting is a technique adored by knitters who love to build dramatic colorscapes with yarn. Our *Creative Color* collection embraces the heritage of Fair Isle while delivering modern, stunning colorwork projects. You'll turn heads with this color-saturated collection of garments and accessories, and stop your admirers in their tracks when they find out you've made these gorgeous items yourself!

Creative Color: 2016 Fair Isle Collection by Knit Picks includes patterns for novice Fair Isle knitters as well as experts. Newcomers can try out colorwork by knitting the Cassia Hat and Mitts or the Flower Island Cardigan. Those already in love with the elegant and subtle shadings of Fair Isle will be delighted by the scarves, hats, pullovers, cardigans and accessories - all beautifully photographed and elegantly written.

Whether you're adding a pop of Fair Isle flair with the Silia Hat or stopping traffic with the Londonderry Jacket, you'll find many patterns to love in this gorgeous collection. Choose your color palette and get started on your journey to Fair Isle without ever leaving home.

HAPPILY SWEATER

by Katy Banks

FINISHED MEASUREMENTS

34 (38, 42, 46, 50.25)" finished bust measurement; garment is meant to be worn with 4" of positive ease.

YARN

Knit Picks Palette (100% Peruvian Highland Wool; 231 yards/50g): C1 Rose Hip 24556, 4 (4, 4, 4, 5) balls; C2 Salsa Heather 24003, C3 Hollyberry 25539, and C4 Currant 24564, 1 ball each; C5 Regal 25089, 2 (2, 2, 2, 3) balls; C6 White 23728, 2 balls.

NEEDLES

US 4 (3.5mm) 24" circular needles plus DPNs or another 24" circular needle for two circulars technique, or size to obtain gauge.

NOTIONS

Yarn Needle
Stitch Marker
Scrap Yarn or Stitch Holders

GAUGE

24 sts and 28 rows = 4" in stranded St st in the round, blocked.

24 sts and 36 rows = 4" in St st in the round, blocked.

Happily Sweater

Notes:

This pullover is worked in the round from the bottom up. Sleeves and body are joined at the underarm and a circular yoke is worked up to the neckline. The background gradient shifts to darker and darker colors as the foreground Fair Isle motif is centered vertically just below the bust. Read each chart row from right to left, as a RS row.

Seed Stitch (in the round over an even number of sts)
Rnd 1: (K1, P1) to end.
Rnd 2: (P1, K1) to end.
Repeat Rnds 1-2 for pattern.

DIRECTIONS
Body

With C1, CO 204 (228, 252, 276, 302) sts, PM to denote beginning of rnd and the right side, and join for working in the round being careful not to twist sts. Work Seed Stitch until piece measures 2" from CO. As you work the last of these rnds, place M at halfway point to denote left side; that is, after 102 (114, 126, 138, 151) sts. Read ahead as shaping and Body Chart are worked simultaneously. Note that some shaping that is described here is also shown on the chart. Work the next rnd as follows.

Body Decrease Rnd: *K1, SSK, K to 3 sts before M, K2tog, K1*, SM, repeat from * to * once more to end of rnd. 4 sts dec.

Work 8 (5, 5, 5, 12) rnds even. Repeat the last 9 (6, 6, 6, 13) rnds 5 (7, 8, 8, 3) times more. 180 (196, 216, 240, 286) sts on needles. Work 15 (9, 19, 17, 16) rnds even. Work the next rnd as follows.

Body Increase Rnd: * K2, M1L, K to 2 sts before M, M1R, K2*, SM, repeat from * to * once more to end of rnd. 4 sts inc.

Work 6 (5, 3, 3, 7) rnds even. Repeat the last 7 (6, 4, 4, 8) rnds 5 (7, 8, 8, 3) times more. Begin Body Chart on the 3rd (4th, 4th, 4th, 4th) rnd after the 2nd (3rd, 1st, 1st, 1st) Body Increase Rnd. 204 (228, 252, 276, 302) sts on needles.

After completing increases, continue to work Body Chart even until you have completed all 51 rnds. Place all sts and markers on scrap yarn or stitch holder(s) and set aside.

Sleeves

With C1, CO 52 (56, 60, 66, 66) sts, PM to denote beginning of rnd, and join for working in the round being careful not to twist sts. Work Seed Stitch for 18 rnds. Change to St st (K every st, every rnd) and work 5 (9, 9, 2, 3) rnds even. Read ahead as shaping and Sleeve Chart are worked simultaneously. Note that some shaping that is described here is also shown on the chart. Work the next rnd as follows.

Sleeve Increase Rnd: K2, M1L, K to 2 sts before M, M1R, K2. 2 sts inc.

Work 10 (10, 10, 11, 5) rnds even. Repeat the last 11 (11, 11, 12, 6) rnds 11 (11, 11, 11, 22) times more. Sizes 34 (38, 42, 46): begin Sleeve Chart on the 11th (11th, 11th, 4th, -) Rnd after the 8th (8th, 8th, 9th, -) Sleeve Increase Rnd. Size 50.25: begin Sleeve Chart on the 18th Sleeve Increase Rnd. 76 (80, 84, 90, 112) sts on needles. After

completing increases, continue to work Sleeve Chart even until you have completed all 51 rnds. Place all sts and M on scrap yarn or stitch holder(s). Repeat for second sleeve.

Yoke

Return sts to needles as follows. Beginning at right side M of Body and with Rnd 1 of the Yoke Chart, keep 6 (6, 7, 8, 8) sts on scrap yarn or holder, place next 90 (101, 112, 122, 135) sts on needle, keep the next 12 (13, 14, 16, 16) sts on scrap yarn or holder, removing the M in the middle of these sts. Beginning at M of one Sleeve, keep 6 (6, 7, 8, 8) sts on scrap yarn or holder, place next 64 (67, 70, 74, 96) sts on needle, keep remaining 6 (7, 7, 8, 8) sts on scrap yarn or holder. Place next 90 (101, 112, 122, 135) sts of Body on needle, keep the remaining 6 (7, 7, 8, 8) sts on scrap yarn or holder. Beginning at M of the remaining Sleeve, keep 6 (7, 7, 8, 8) sts on scrap yarn or holder, place next 64 (67, 70, 74, 96) sts on needle, keep remaining 6 (6, 7, 8, 8) sts on scrap yarn or holder. Place M here, rnds begin and end at the back of the right shoulder. 308 (336, 364, 392, 462) sts on needles. Continue through all rnds of the Yoke Chart, slipping the first st of each rnd P-wise WYIB and moving M to after this st. This moves M one st to the left on each rnd, eliminating the jog in the motif that would otherwise occur at the transition between rnds. Notice that the chart has a line indicating where the moving M is located. Break C1, continue with C5 to end.

Dec Rnd 1: *K4, K2tog; rep from * to the last 2 (0, 4, 2, 0) sts, K to the end. 257 (280, 304, 327, 385) sts on needles. Work 9 (10, 12, 13, 14) rnds even.

Dec Rnd 2: *K3, K2tog; rep from * 25 (28, 30, 32, 38) times, K 2 (0, 4, 2, 0), work *K3, K2tog; rep from * to the end. 206 (224, 244, 262, 308) sts on needles. Work 9 (10, 11, 12, 13) rnds even.

Dec Rnd 3: *K2, K2tog; rep from * to the last 2 (0, 0, 2, 0) sts, K to the end. 155 (168, 183, 197, 231) sts on needles. Work 8 (9, 10, 11, 12) rnds even.

Dec Rnd 4: *K2, K2tog; rep from * 19 (21, 22, 24, 28) times, K3 (0, 3, 1, 3), work *K2, K2tog; rep from * to the end. 117 (126, 138, 148, 174) sts on needle. Size 50.25 ONLY, work 4 rnds even.

Dec Rnd 5: *K35 (29, 21, 35, 19) K2tog; rep from * to the last 6 (2, 0, 0, 6) sts, K to the end. 114 (122, 132, 144, 166) sts on needles. Work 0 (2, 2, 4, 4) rnds even. Work 1" in Seed Stitch. BO loosely.

Finishing

Graft underarms using Kitchener Stitch. Weave in ends, wash and block to diagram.

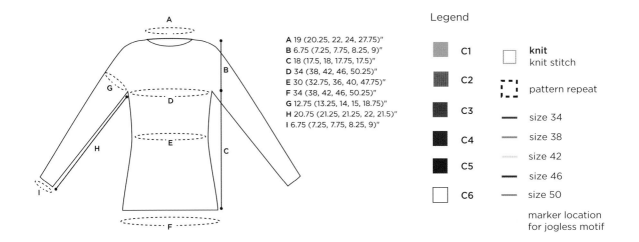

Legend

A 19 (20.25, 22, 24, 27.75)"
B 6.75 (7.25, 7.75, 8.25, 9)"
C 18 (17.5, 18, 17.75, 17.5)"
D 34 (38, 42, 46, 50.25)"
E 30 (32.75, 36, 40, 47.75)"
F 34 (38, 42, 46, 50.25)"
G 12.75 (13.25, 14, 15, 18.75)"
H 20.75 (21.25, 21.25, 22, 21.5)"
I 6.75 (7.25, 7.75, 8.25, 9)"

	C1		knit knit stitch
	C2		pattern repeat
	C3		size 34
	C4		size 38
	C5		size 42
	C6		size 46
			size 50

marker location
for jogless motif

Front and Back Chart

Sleeve Chart

Yoke Chart

14	13	12	11	10	9	8	7	6	5	4	3	2	1	
														16
														15
														14
														13
														12
														11
														10
														9
														8
														7
														6
														5
														4
														3
														2
														1	joining round

LAVER SCARF

by Kate Heppell

FINISHED MEASUREMENTS
10" wide (20" circumference) x 80" long

YARN
Knit Picks Palette (100% Peruvian Highland Wool; 231 yards/50g): A Oyster Heather 24559, B Mongoose 25084, C Grizzly Heather 25532, E Teal 24000, F Spruce 25535, G Cornmeal 24252, H Masala 24248, 1 ball each. D Celadon Heather 24254, I Garnet Heather 24015, 2 balls each.

NEEDLES
US 2 (3mm) DPNs (for grafting) and/or two 24" circular needles for two circulars technique, or one 32" or longer circular needle for Magic Loop technique, or size to obtain gauge

NOTIONS
Yarn Needle
Stitch Markers

GAUGE
28 sts and 32 rows = 4" over stranded St st in the rnd, blocked.

Laver Scarf

Notes:

This scarf is worked in the round. For a seamless finish, it begins with Judy's Magic Cast On and finishes with Kitchener Stitch. Yarns not in use can either be carried up the inside of the work or broken off and woven in as you go, whichever you prefer. These ends will all be hidden inside the scarf.

Follow each row of the chart from right to left, repeating the chart ten times across the round.

Judy's Magic Cast On

http://tutorials.knitpicks.com/wptutorials/judys-magic-cast-on/

Kitchener Stitch

http://tutorials.knitpicks.com/wptutorials/kelleys-sock-class-kitchener-stitch/

DIRECTIONS

Scarf

Using Judy's Magic Cast On and A, CO 140 sts, PM for beginning of rnd.

Work Rnds 1-92 of Laver Chart 6 times, then work Rnds 1-89 once.

Next Rnd: With A, knit.

Break yarn, leaving a long tail for grafting.

Finishing

Weave in ends. Arrange sts evenly onto DPNs, in two pairs of 70 sts. Graft the ends using Kitchener Stitch and A. Weave in remaining ends, wash and block.

Laver Chart

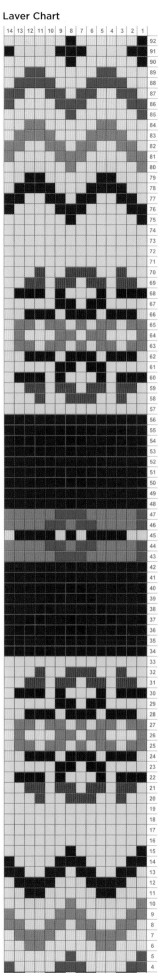

Legend

☐	**knit** knit stitch
	A
	B
	C
	D
	E
	F
	G
	H
	I

LONDONDERRY JACKET

by Anne Podlesak

 For pattern support, contact anne.podlesak@gmail.com

FINISHED MEASUREMENTS.

32.5 (36.5, 40.75, 44.25, 48.5, 52.5, 56.75, 60.75, 64.5)" finished bust/waist measurement with garment buttoned closed at waistline; garment is meant to be worn with 1-2" of positive ease at the bust.

YARN

Knit Picks Palette (100% Peruvian Highland Wool; 231 yards/50g): MC Garnet Heather 24015, 5 (5, 6, 7, 8, 9, 11, 12, 13) balls; C1 Brindle Heather 24004, 2 (2, 3, 3, 4, 4, 5, 5, 6) balls; C2 Rose Hip 24556, 1 (1, 1, 2, 2, 2, 2, 3, 3) balls; C3 Oyster Heather 24559, 1 (1, 1, 2, 2, 2, 2, 3, 3) balls; C4 Brass Heather 25542, 1 (1, 2, 2, 3, 3, 4, 4, 5) balls; C5 Clarity 25548, 1 (1, 1, 2, 2, 2, 2, 3, 3) balls; C6 Wheat Heather 26056, 2 (2, 3, 3, 4, 4, 5, 5, 6) balls; C7 Merlot Heather 24014, 1 (1, 3, 3, 4, 4, 5, 5, 6) balls; C8 Autumn Heather 24002, 2 (2, 3, 3, 4, 4, 5, 5, 6) balls; C9 Cornmeal 24252, 1 (1, 1, 2, 2, 2, 2, 3, 3) balls.

NEEDLES

US 3 (3.25mm) 32" and 40" or longer circular needles, plus DPN's or preferred method to work in the round, or size to obtain gauge.

NOTIONS

Yarn Needle
Stitch Markers
Scrap Yarn or Stitch Holder
Seven 0.5" Buttons
Contrasting Bright Sewing Thread
Optional (for sewn steeks): 0.25" Grosgrain Ribbon measuring the length of the steek openings and neck band for your size, plus 6".

GAUGE

29 sts and 38 rows = 4" in stranded and unstranded St st in the round, blocked.

Londonderry Jacket

Notes:

This duster-style jacket is knit in the round from the bottom hem up to the armholes. The sleeves are then knit in the round, and then joined to the body to be worked back and forth while shaping the V-neckline. The sleeves and upper body are worked with raglan shaping. Once the body and sleeves are complete, the lower portion is cut open along the steeks, which are then trimmed, sewn down and finished with an optional grosgrain ribbon. The seed stitch front bands are then picked up and knit.

Be sure to check your gauge over both the stockinette and stranded/colorwork portions of this garment. Many knitters will need to go up a needle size on the colorwork portions to ensure their gauge remains the same throughout.

When working the 8-stitch steek, always work the stitches closest to the body of the sweater in either the MC (for the non-stranded knitting portion) or in the background contrast color. When working the remaining steek stitches in the colorwork portion, alternate the contrast colors being used in a checkerboard fashion, i.e., 1 stitch of each color, alternating. Change colors at the beginning of round marker.

The charts are read from right to left on all rounds, and are worked in the round. When beginning Round 1 of a chart, break MC, and then attach and break off contrast colors as needed at the beginning of round marker.

You may choose to work the steeks in any fashion you wish. I opted to do a sewn/reinforced steek. To do this, hand-baste a bright colored sewing thread between the stitches on either side of the beginning of round marker. Then machine sew 1 stitch away from this sewing thread to prevent any raveling of the edges when cutting along the bright colored sewing thread to separate the fronts of the jacket. Trim any loose yarn ends flush with the machine-sewn edge to reduce bulk. Optional: Use a narrow (0.25") ribbon to cover the cut ends, whip-stitching the ribbon into place once the front bands are completed and buttons are sewn on.

Stockinette Stitch (St st, worked flat over any number of sts)
Row1 (RS): K all sts.
Row 2 (WS): P all sts.
Rep Rows 1-2 for pattern.

Stockinette Stitch (St st, worked in the round over any number of sts)
All Rnds: K all stitches.

Moss Stitch (worked flat or in the round over an even number of sts):
Row/Rnd 1 (RS): *K1, P1; rep from * to end of rnd.
Row/Rnd 2 (WS): *P1, K1; rep from * to end of rnd.
Rep Rows/Rnds 1-2 for pattern.

DIRECTIONS
Sleeves (make 2 the same)
The sleeves are worked in the round from the wrists up to the armholes.

Hem
Loosely CO 56 (56, 60, 60, 64, 64, 68, 68, 72) sts using DPNs or preferred method for working in the rnd, using MC. PM and join, being careful not to twist sts.

Moss Stitch
Work Moss Stitch for a total of 6 (6, 8, 8, 8, 8, 10, 10, 10) rds.

K 1 rnd.
Work Rnds 1-5 of Chart A.

First Increase Rnd, using MC:
For sizes 40.75 (44.25)" ONLY: K8, M1, (K15, M1) 3 times, K7. 64 sts.
For sizes 48.5 (52.5)" ONLY: K4, M1, (K8, M1) 7 times, K4. 72 sts.
For sizes 56.75 (60.75)" ONLY: K14, M1, (K13, M1) 3 times, K15. 72 sts.

All Sizes: K 2 (2, 1, 1, 1, 1, 1, 1, 2) rnds with MC.
Work Rnds 1-19 of Chart B.
Knit 1 round in MC.

Second Increase Rnd, using MC:
For sizes 32.5 (36.5)" ONLY: K7, M1, (K14, M1) 3 times, K7. 60 sts.
For sizes 40.75 (44.25)" ONLY: K8, M1, (K16, M1) 3 times, K8. 68 sts.
For sizes 56.75 (60.75, 64.5)" ONLY: K4, M1, (K9, M1) 7 times, K5. 80 sts.

All Sizes: K 1 (1, 1, 1, 2, 2, 1, 1, 1) rnds in MC.
Work Rnds 3-5 of Chart A.
K 1 rnd in MC.

Third Increase Rnd, using MC:
For sizes 32.5 (36.5)" ONLY: K8, M1, (K15, M1) 3 times, K7. 64 sts.
For sizes 40.75 (44.25)" ONLY: K8, M1, (K17, M1) 3 times, K9. 72 sts.
For sizes 48.5 (52.5)" ONLY: K9, M1 (K18, M1) 3 times, K9. 76 sts.
All Sizes: K 1 (1, 1, 1, 1, 1, 2, 2, 2,)rnds in MC.
Work Rnds 1-33 of Chart C1 or C2 as noted for your size.
K 1 rnd in MC.

Fourth Increase Rnd, using MC:
For sizes 32.5 (36.5)" ONLY: K8, M1, (K16, M1) 3 times, K8. 68 sts.
For sizes 40.75 (44.25)" ONLY: K9, M1, (K18, M1) 3 times, K9. 76 sts.
For sizes 48.5 (52.5)" ONLY: K9, M1, (K19, M1) 3 times, K10. 80 sts.
For sizes 56.75 (60.75, 64.5)" ONLY: K10, M1, (K20, M1) 3 times, K10. 84 sts.
All Sizes: K 1 rnd in MC.
Work Rnds 3-6 of Chart A.

Fifth Increase Rnd, using MC:
For sizes 32.5 (36.5)" ONLY: K9, M1 (K17, M1) 3 times, K8. 72 sts.
For sizes 40.75 (44.25)" ONLY: K9, M1, (K19, M1) 3 times, K10. 80 sts.
For sizes 48.5 (52.5)" ONLY: K5, M1, (K10, M1) 7 times, K5. 88 sts.
For sizes 56.75 (60.75, 64.5)" ONLY: K4, M1, (K7, M1) 11 times, K3. 96 sts.
All Sizes: K1 rnd in MC.
Work Rnds 1-19 of Chart B.
K1 rnd in MC.

Sixth Increase Rnd, using MC:
For sizes 32.5 (36.5)" ONLY: K9, M1, (K18, M1) 3 times, K9. 76 sts.
For sizes 40.75 (44.25)" ONLY: K10, M1, (K20, M1) 3 times, K10. 84 sts.
For sizes 48.5 (52.5)" ONLY: K11, M1, (K22, M1) 3 times, K11. 92 sts.
For sizes 56.75 (60.75, 64.5)" ONLY: K6, M1, (K12, M1) 7 times, K6. 104 sts.
All Sizes: Work Rnds 3-6 of Chart A.

Seventh Increase Rnd, using MC:
For sizes 32.5 (36.5)" ONLY: K10, M1, (K19, M1) 3 times, K9. 80 sts.
For sizes 40.75 (44.25)" ONLY: K10, M1, (K21, M1) 3 times, K11. 88 sts.
For sizes 48.5 (52.5)" ONLY: K11, M1, (K23, M1) 3 times, K12. 96 sts.
For sizes 56.75 (60.75, 64.5)" ONLY: K7, M1, (K15, M1) 6 times, K7, M1. 112 sts.
All Sizes: K4 (5, 4, 2, 2, 2, 2, 2) rnds with MC.

Sleeve Increase Rnd: K1, M1, K to 1 st before end of rnd, M1, K1. 2 sts inc.
Work a Sleeve Increase Rnd, followed by 4 (5, 4, 2, 1, 1, 1, 1) rnds as established a total of 7 (7, 10, 16, 17, 22, 20, 22, 25) times. 94 (94, 108, 120, 130, 140, 152, 156, 162) sts.

Continue to work St st in the rnd until sleeve measures 17 (18, 18.25, 18.25, 18.25, 18.25, 18.5, 19, 19.5)" or desired length from CO edge of cuff, ending 7 (7, 8, 9, 10 12, 14, 16, 18) sts before the end of the rnd. BO the next 14 (14, 16, 18, 20, 24, 28, 32, 36) sts, then work to end of rnd. 80 (80, 92, 102, 110, 116, 124, 124, 126) sts.
Move sleeve sts to scrap yarn or spare needle, and place on hold.

Body

Hem

Loosely CO 296 (328, 360, 392, 392, 424, 456, 488, 520) sts using long circular needles and MC. Place contrasting marker for beginning of rnd, and place 2 other markers, one 4 sts before beginning of rnd and one 4 sts after beginning of rnd to mark edges of steek sts. Knit all 8 steek sts on every round (see Notes section for more information).

Work Moss Stitch for a total of 8 (8, 10, 10, 12, 12, 14, 14, 14) rnds, working 8 steek sts as knit sts.
K 1 rnd with MC.

Work Rows 1-7 of Chart A, breaking off and attaching CCs at beginning of rnd, and working steek sts in alternating CC colors.
Work Rnds 1-19 of Chart B.
Work Rnds 1-5 of Chart A.

On the next rnd, with MC, K4 steek sts, SM, K to 5 sts before end of rnd, M1, K1, SM, K4 steek sts. 297 (329, 361, 393, 393, 425, 457, 489, 521) sts.
K 1 rnd with MC.
Work Rnds 1-33 of Chart D.

On the next round, with MC, K4 steek sts, SM, K to 6 sts before end of rnd, K2tog, K1, SM, K4 steek sts. 296 (328, 360, 392, 392, 424, 456, 488, 520) sts.
K 1 rnd with MC.
Work Rnds 3-7 of Chart A.
Work Rnds 1-19 of Chart B.
Work Rnds 1-5 of Chart A.

On the next rnd, with MC, K4 steek sts, SM, K to 5 sts before end of rnd, M1, K1, SM, K4 steek sts. 297 (329, 361, 393, 393, 425, 457, 489, 521) sts.
K 1 rnd with MC.
Work Rnds 1-33 of Chart D.
On the next rnd, with MC, K4 steek sts, SM, K to 7 sts before end of rnd, K2tog, K1, SM, K4 steek sts. 296 (328, 360, 392, 392, 424, 456, 488, 520) sts.

First Decrease Round (with MC):
Size 32.5": K4 steek sts, SM, K11, K2tog, (K22, K2tog) 11 times, K11, SM, K4 steek sts. 276 sts + 8 steek sts; 284 sts.
Size 36.5": K4 sts, SM, K6, K2tog, (K42, K2tog) 7 times, K4, SM, K4 steek sts. 312 sts + 8 steek sts; 320 sts.
Size 40.75": K4 steek sts, SM, K10, K2tog, (K20, K2tog) 15 times, K10, SM, K4 steek sts. 336 sts + 8 steek sts; 344 sts.
Size 44.25": K4 steek sts, SM, K11, K2tog, (K22, K2tog) 15 times, K11, SM, K4 steek sts. 368 sts + 8 steek sts; 376 sts.
Size 48.5": K4 steek sts, SM, K23, K2tog, (K46, K2tog) 7 times, K23, SM, K4 steek sts. 376 sts + 8 steek sts; 384 sts.
Size 52.5": K4 steek sts, SM, K25, K2tog, (K50, K2tog) 7 times, K25, SM, K4 steek sts. 408 + 8 steek sts; 416 sts.
Size 56.75": K4 steek sts, SM, K20, K2tog, (K35, K2tog) 11 times, K19, SM, K4 steek sts. 436 + 8 steek sts; 444 sts.
Size 60.75": K4 steek sts, SM, K19, K2tog, (K38, K2tog) 11 times, K19, SM, K4 steek sts. 468 + 8 steek sts; 476 sts.
Size 64.5": K4 steek sts, SM, K19, K2tog, (K41, K2tog) 11 times, K18, SM, K4 steek sts. 500 + 8 steek sts; 508 sts.
Work Rnds 3-5 of Chart A.
K 1 rnd with MC.

Second Decrease Round (with MC):
Size 32.5": K4 steek sts, SM, K11, K2tog, (K21, K2tog) 11 times, K10, SM, K4 steek sts. 264 sts + 8 steek sts; 272 sts.
Size 36.5": K4 steek sts, SM, K12, K2tog, (K17, K2tog) 15 times, K13, SM, K4 steek sts. 296 sts + 8 steek sts; 304 sts.
Size 40.75": K4 steek sts, SM, K10, K2tog, (K19, K2tog) 15 times, K9, SM, K4 steek sts. 320 + 8 steek sts; 328 sts.
Size 44.25": K4 steek sts, SM, K11, K2tog, (K21, K2tog) 15 times, K10, SM, K4 steek sts. 352 + 8 steek sts; 360 sts.
Size 48.5": K4 steek sts, SM, K7, K2tog, (K22, K2tog) 15 times, K7, SM, K4 steek sts. 360 + 8 steek sts; 368 sts.
Size 52.5": K4 steek sts, SM, K8, K2tog, (K24, K2tog) 15 times, K8, SM, K4 steek sts. 392 + 8 steek sts; 400 sts.
Size 56.75": K4 steek sts, SM, K19, K2tog, (K34, K2tog) 11 times, K19, SM, K4 steek sts. 424 + 8 steek sts; 432 sts.
Size 60.75": K4 steek sts, SM, K18, K2tog, (K37, K2tog) 11 times, K19, SM, K4 steek sts. 456 + 8 steek sts; 464 sts.
Size 64.5": K4 steek sts, SM, K18, K2tog, (K40, K2tog) 11 times, K18, SM, K4 steek sts. 488 + 8 steek sts; 496 sts.
All Sizes: On the next round, K 1 rnd with MC.
Work Rnds 1-19 of Chart B again.
K 1 rnd with MC.

Third Decrease Round (with MC):
Size 32.5": K4 steek sts, SM, K4, K2tog, (K15, K2tog) 15 times, K3, SM, K4 steek sts. 248 + 8 steek sts; 256 sts.
Size 36.5": K4 steek sts, SM, K5, K2tog, (K17, K2tog) 15 times, K4, SM, K4 steek sts. 280 + 8 steek sts; 288 sts.

Size 36.5": K4 steek sts, SM, K5, K2tog, (K17, K2tog) 15 times, K4, SM, K4 steek sts. 280 + 8 steek sts; 288 sts.

Size 40.75": K4 steek sts, SM, K9, K2tog, (K18, K2tog) 15 times, K9, SM, K4 steek sts. 304 + 8 steek sts; 312 sts.

Size 44.25": K4 steek sts, SM, K10, K2tog, (K20, K2tog) 15 times, K10, SM, K4 steek sts. 336 + 8 steek sts; 344 sts.

Size 48.5": K4 steek sts, SM, K44, K2tog, (K88, K2tog) 3 times, K44, SM, K4 steek sts. 356 + 8 steek sts; 364 sts.

Size 52.5": K4 steek sts, SM, K48, K2tog, (K96, K2tog) 3 times, K48, SM, K4 steek sts. 388 + 8 steek sts; 396 sts.

Size 56.75": K4 steek sts, SM, K26, K2tog, (K51, K2tog) 7 times, K25, SM, K4 steek sts. 416 + 8 steek sts; 424 sts.

Size 60.75": K4 steek sts, SM, K24, K2tog, (K35, K2tog) 11 times, K23, SM, K4 steek sts. 444 + 8 steek sts; 452 sts.

Size 64.5": K4 steek sts, SM, K18, K2tog, (K28, K2tog) 15 times, K18, SM, K4 steek sts. 472 + 8 steek sts; 480 sts.

Work Rnds 3-5 of chart A.

K1 round with MC.

Fourth Decrease Round (with MC):

Size 32.5": K4 steek sts, SM, K3, K2tog, (K14, K2tog) 15 times, K3, SM, K4 steek sts. 232 + 8 steek sts; 240 sts.

Size 36.5": K4 steek sts; SM, K6, K2tog, (K12, K2tog) 19 times, K6, SM, K4 steek sts. 260 + 8 steek sts; 268 sts.

Size 40.75": K4 steek sts, SM, K14, K2tog, (K23, K2tog) 11 times, K13, SM, K4 steek sts. 292 + 8 steek sts; 300 sts.

Size 44.25": K4 steek sts, SM, K6, K2tog, (K15, K2tog) 19 times, K5, SM, K4 steek sts. 316 + 8 steek sts; 324 sts.

Size 48.5": K4 steek sts, SM, K20, K2tog, (K43, K2tog) 7 times, K19, SM, K4 steek sts. 348 + 8 steek sts; 356 sts.

Size 52.5": K4 steek sts, SM, K11, K2tog, (K31, K2tog) 11 times, K12, SM, K4 steek sts. 376 + 8 steek sts; 384 sts

Size 56.75": K4 steek sts, SM, K25, K2tog, (K50, K2tog) 7 times, K25, SM, K4 steek sts. 416 + 8 steek sts; 416 sts.

Size 60.75": K4 steek sts, SM, K25, K2tog, (K54, K2tog) 7 times, K25, SM, K4 steek sts. 436 + 8 steek sts; 444 sts.

Size 64.5": K4 steek sts, SM, K29, K2tog, (K57, K2tog) 7 times, K28, SM, K4 steek sts. 464 + 8 steek sts; 472 sts.

Continue to work in the round as established using MC and maintaining 8 steek sts at center front until body measures 7.5 (7.5, 7.75, 8, 8, 8.5, 8.5, 8.75, 9)" from Fourth Decrease Round, or desired length to underarm.

On the next round, BO 4 steek sts, remove marker, K51 (58, 65, 70, 77, 82, 88, 93, 98), BO 14 (14, 16, 18, 20, 24, 28, 32, 36) sts, K102 (116, 130, 140, 154, 164, 176, 186, 196), BO 14 (14, 16, 18, 20, 24, 28, 32, 36) sts, K51 (58, 65, 70, 77, 82, 88, 93, 98), remove marker, BO 4 steek sts. 204 (232, 260, 280, 308, 328, 352, 372, 392) sts.

Join Body and Sleeves

Note that garment will be worked back and forth in St st on circular needles from this point on and that stitch counts will no longer include the 8 steek sts since those were bound off on the prior round.

Next Row (RS): (RS), K51 (58, 65, 70, 77, 82, 88, 93, 98) of right front, PM, K80 (80, 92, 102, 110, 116, 124, 124, 126) sts of right sleeve, PM, K102 (116, 130, 140, 154, 164, 176, 186, 196) sts of back, PM, K80 (80, 92, 102, 110, 116, 124, 124, 126) sts of left sleeve, PM, K51 (58, 65, 70, 77, 82, 88, 93, 98) of left front. 364 (392, 444, 484, 528, 560, 600, 620, 644) sts.

Work 3 rows in St st.

Raglan Decreases and Neckline Decreases occur at the same time. Read through instructions before proceeding.

Raglan Decrease Row (RS): *K to 3 sts before M, SSK, K1, SM, K1, K2tog; rep from * to end of row, K to end. 8 sts dec.

Double Raglan Decrease Row (RS): *K to 3 sts before right sleeve M, SSK, K1, SM, K1, K3tog; K to 4 sts before right back M, SSSK, K1, SM, K1, K3tog; K to 4 sts before left back M, SSSK, K1, SM, K1, K3tog; K to 4 sts before left sleeve M, SSSK, K1, SM, K1, K2tog, K to end of row. 14 sts dec.

Work a Double Raglan Decrease Row every RS row 3 (3, 4, 5, 6, 7, 8, 9, 10) times. On the following (WS) row, work in St st as established.

On the next row (RS), work a Raglan Decrease Row. On the following (WS) row, work in St st as established.

Then, continue to work a RS Raglan Decrease Row 31 (33, 36, 39, 40, 41, 41, 42, 41) times, followed by a St st row on the WS until 56 (68, 72, 74, 92, 98, 112, 106, 124) sts remain. (Neckline Shaping will be completed before Raglan Decreases.) Remove all markers on final WS row.

AT THE SAME TIME, after working the first 8 Decrease Rows, also begin working a Neckline Decrease Row thusly:

Neckline Decrease Row (RS): K1, SSK, work to last 3 sts as established, K2tog, K1. 2 sts dec.

Work a Neckline Decrease Row a total of 5 (5, 10, 10, 12, 14, 20, 22, 22) times every 4th (4th, 2nd, 2nd, 2nd, 2nd, 2nd, 2nd, 2nd) RS row, while continuing to work the Raglan Decrease Rows.

Note when working size 36.5 ONLY, when working the final Raglan Decrease (which will leave you with 0 sts for the sleeves), you will need to work the final decrease thusly: Work the right front as established with Raglan Decreases to the right sleeve marker, SM, SSK, K2tog, then SM and work the back with Raglan Decreases as established, slip the left sleeve marker, SSK, K2tog, SM, and then work to the end of the row, working Raglan Decrease for the left front as established.

You will have 11 (16, 14, 15, 18, 19, 18, 19, 24) sts for each front half, 4 (0, 2, 2, 4, 4, 8, 2, 2) sts for each sleeve, and 26 (36, 40, 40, 48, 52, 60, 64, 72) sts for the back remaining on the needles. 56 (68, 72, 74, 92, 98, 112, 106, 124) sts. Place sts on hold.

Front Steeks

You may choose to finish the steeks by any method of your choice. If you wish to use the sewn steek method I used: Using either a hand-sewn or machine sewn-running stitch and sewing thread, stitch along the edges of each front steek, about 2 sts away from the central line. Then, using sharp scissors, cut open the steek along the center line, and trim any loose ends. Fold each steek to the inside of the front of the garment along the line formed between the steek sts and the garment, and using sewing thread, tack the loose edges of the steeks to the inside of the garment. Cut a length of .025" grosgrain ribbon approximately 12" longer than the length from the bottom of the right hem measured along the inside of the jacket, around the neckline, and down to the bottom of the left hem. Turn under one end of the ribbon and position it so it is a scant 1/8" from the bottom right hem inside edge. Using sewing thread, whip stitch the grosgrain ribbon along both of its edges to cover the cut edges of the steeks, easing the ribbon as necessary around the inside curve of the back neck. When the left lower hem is reached, trim the ribbon to the appropriate length, leaving enough to turn under and positioning it a scant 1/8 " from the bottom inside edge of the left hem and finish tacking in place.

Front Bands/Neckband

Mark spacing of buttonhole placement along right front of garment, placing one buttonhole centered over the final repeat of Chart A at the waist, and then 3 buttonholes evenly spaced above this central point to the bottom edge of the V-neckline, and 3 more buttonholes below the central point of Chart A, evenly spaced to match those above the central point.

Using MC and longer circular needle, and with RS side of the garment facing you, PU and K 4 out of every 5 sts along the right edge of the sweater, K56 (68, 72, 74, 92, 98, 112, 106, 124) live sts of neck and back remaining on the needles, then PU and K 4 out of every 5 sts along the left edge of the sweater, making sure to have an odd number of sts when all sts have been worked.

Work 3 rows of Seed Stitch, ending with a WS row. On the next row, work buttonholes thusly: *Work to marked spot of buttonhole, YO, K2tog; repeat from * and then work to end of button band in Seed st as established. On the next row (WS), work in Seed St as established, and when reaching the buttonholes created on the prior row, work the YO stitch in Seed st pattern as established. Work 3 more rows of Seed St, ending with a RS row. BO all sts on the WS LOOSELY in knit.

Finishing

Graft underarm seams. Attach buttons on the left front of the jacket on the button bands, across from the right button band buttonholes. Weave in ends, wash and block to diagram.

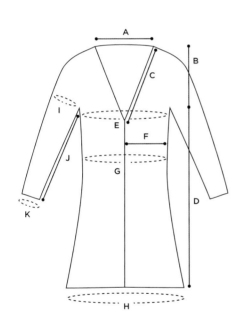

A 4 (5, 5.5, 5.5, 6.5, 7.25, 8.25, 8.75, 10)"
B 8 (8.5, 9.25, 10, 105, 11, 11, 11.5, 11.5)"
C 5.75 (6.25, 7, 7.75, 8.25, 8.75, 8.75, 9.25, 9.25)"
D 28 (28, 28.25, 28.5, 28.5, 28.5, 29, 29.25, 29.5)"
E 32.5 (36.5, 40.75, 45.25, 48.5, 52.75, 60.75, 64.5)"
F 16.25 (18.25, 20.5, 22, 24.5, 26.25, 28.5, 32.25)"
G 32.5 (36.5, 40.75, 45.25, 48.5, 52.75, 60.75, 64.5)"
H 40.25 (44.75, 49, 53.5, 53.5, 58, 62.25, 66.75, 71.25)"
I 13 (13, 15, 16.5, 18, 19.25, 21, 21.5, 22.25)"
J 17 (18, 18.5, 18.25, 18.25, 18.25, 18.5, 19, 19.5)"
K 7.75 (7.75, 8.25, 8.25, 8.75, 8.75, 9.25, 9.25, 10)"

Chart B

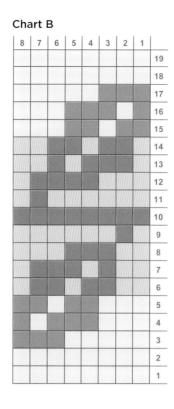

Chart A

Legend

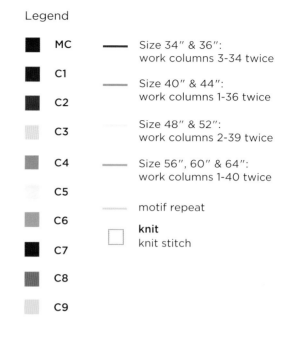

■	MC
■	C1
■	C2
▦	C3
▦	C4
▦	C5
▦	C6
■	C7
▦	C8
▦	C9

—— Size 34" & 36":
work columns 3-34 twice

—— Size 40" & 44":
work columns 1-36 twice

—— Size 48" & 52":
work columns 2-39 twice

—— Size 56", 60" & 64":
work columns 1-40 twice

······· motif repeat

□ **knit**
knit stitch

Chart C1

Chart C2

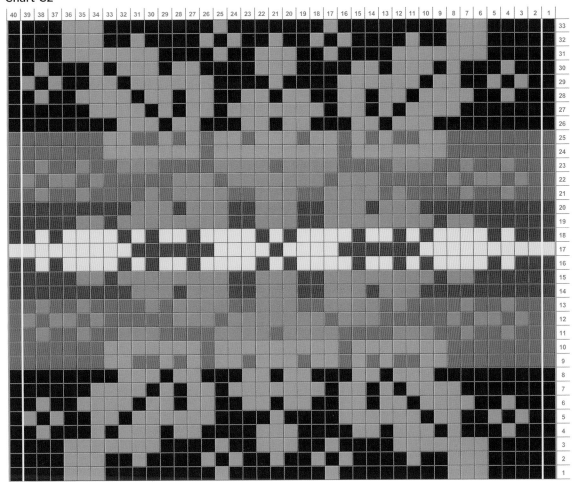

Chart D

MILLEFIORI

by Cristina Ghirlanda

FINISHED MEASUREMENTS

21.25" circumference, buttoned, and 12.75" high, folded

YARN

Knit Picks Palette (100% Peruvian Highland Wool; 231 yards/50g):
MC Regal 25089, 2 balls; C1 Pennyroyal 25090, C2 Marine Heather 24010, C3 Clarity 25548; 1 ball each.

NEEDLES

US 2 (2.75mm) 16" circular needle, or size to obtain gauge
US 1 (2.5mm) any length circular needle, or one size smaller than needle to obtain gauge, for band

NOTIONS

Yarn Needle
8 Buttons 5/8" diameter
Spare US 2 (2.75mm) or smaller size circular needle, any length

GAUGE

30 sts and 33 rows = 4" in stranded St st in the round on larger needle, blocked.
26 sts and 40 rows = 4" in Garter st on smaller needle, blocked.

Millefiori

Read all charts from the right to the left. All squares are knit stitches.

The color dominance is ordered as follows (from the most dominant to the least): MC, C2, C3, C1. Hold the more dominant color to the left, independent of your knitting style.

At the beginning of each round, place unused colors to your right to avoid tangling.

Twist C2 with MC at the beginning of Round 5 and Round 11 of Millefiori Chart to bring C2 up.

You may wish to place markers every 16 sts (4 pattern repeats) to make it easier to follow the chart.

DIRECTIONS

With larger needle and C2, use the Provisional Method to CO 192 sts.

Join and begin working in the round, being careful not to twist sts.

Work in Millefiori Chart around from Round 1 through Round 16 ten times, then work from Round 1 through Round 7 once. Or alternatively, work until piece measures 20.25", ending after Round 7.

Non-buttonhole Band

Transfer 96 sts to spare needle. Flatten the tube. With smaller needle and C2, *K tog first st from the upper layer and first st from the lower layer; rep from * to end. 96 sts.
Work in Garter st (K every row) until band measures 1".
BO all sts K-wise. Cut yarn.

Buttonhole Band

Keeping the tube flat, transfer 96 provisional CO sts to larger needle and transfer the remaining 96 provisional CO sts to spare needle. With smaller needle, join C2, *K tog first st from the upper layer and first st from the lower layer; rep from * to end. 96 sts.
Knit 4 rows.
Next Row (buttonholes): K6, (YO, K2tog, K10) 7 times, YO, K2tog, K4.
Continue in Garter st until band measures 1".
BO all sts K-wise. Cut yarn.

Finishing

Weave in ends, wash and block to measurements. Sew buttons to the Non-buttonhole Band, in line with the buttonholes.

Millefiori Chart

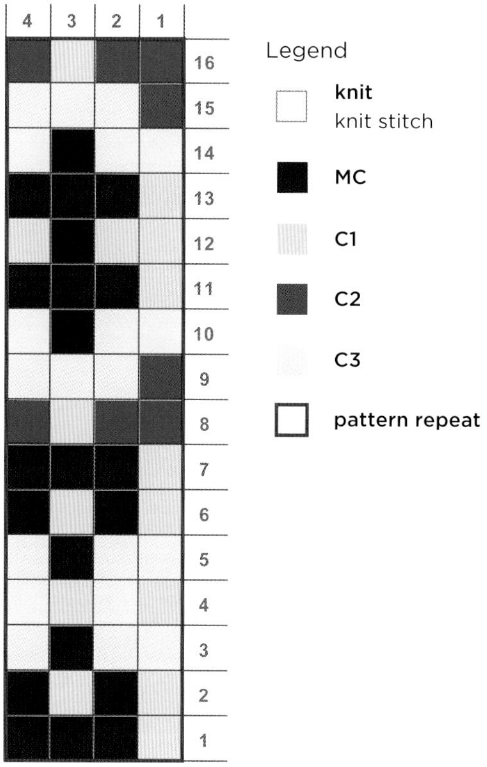

Legend

- knit / knit stitch
- MC
- C1
- C2
- C3
- pattern repeat

CARIVEL COLORBLOCK SWEATER

by Megan Spencer

 For pattern support, contact megan_c_spencer@yahoo.com

FINISHED MEASUREMENTS

32.5 (34, 36.25, 38.25, 40.25, 42.25, 43.75, 48, 52.25)" finished bust measurement; garment is meant to be worn with little to no ease at the bust.

YARN

Knit Picks Palette (100% Peruvian Highland Wool; 231 yards/50g): C1 Marine Heather 24010, C2 Spruce 25535, C3 Tidepool Heather 24007, C5 Teal 24000, C6 Spearmint 24253, C7 Cream 23730, C8 Coriander Heather 25544, C9 Grizzly Heather 25532, C10 Merlot Heather 24014, C12 Fairy Tale 24565; 1 ball each. C4 Aurora Heather 25537 3 (3, 3, 4, 4, 4, 4, 4, 5) balls. C11 Regal 25089 2 (2, 2, 2, 2, 2, 2, 2, 2) balls.

NEEDLES

US 3 (3.25mm) 32" circular needles, plus DPNs or longer circular needles for Magic Loop method, or size to obtain gauge US 2 (3mm) 32" circular needles, plus DPNs or longer circular needles for Magic Loop method, or one size smaller than used to obtain gauge

NOTIONS

Yarn Needle
Sharp-pointed Sewing Needle and matching Thread
8 Stitch Markers, with one different than the others
Scrap Yarn or Stitch Holders

GAUGE

31 sts and 34 rows = 4" in stranded St st on larger needle, in the round, blocked
31 sts and 38 rows = 4" in St st on larger needle, in the round, blocked

Carivel Colorblock Sweater

Notes:

The stranded sweater body is knit in the round from the hem up, until you reach the shoulders. The dropped shoulders are then knit flat, which will require either purling in pattern on the WS of the work or knitting backwards for a few rows. Hem, cuff, and neck edgings are folded stockinette stitch, knit with a purled turning ridge. They are folded and stitched in place during finishing. Steeks are used for the armholes and neck opening. Seven stitch steeks are worked in a birds-eye pattern of alternating colors for stability. Set-in sleeves, knit in single color stockinette stitch, are knit separately from the body. They are worked in the round from the cuff up, until you reach the sleeve cap, which is knit flat.

DIRECTIONS
Body
Bottom Folded Hem

With smaller needles, and C12, CO 264 (280, 296, 312, 328, 340, 356, 388, 416) sts. PM and join to work in the round, being careful not to twist sts. The beginning of the round is the left underarm. Work in St st (K every rnd) for 1.5".

Change to larger needles and purl 1 rnd for the Turning Ridge.

Knit the outside of the folded hem, establishing two lines of purl sts for the side "seams" as follows: *K131 (139, 147, 155, 163, 169, 177, 193, 207), P1; rep from * once more. Repeat this rnd until second side of hem measures 1.5" from turning ridge.

Begin Colorwork Pattern Body

Read the chart from right to left. The purled side "seam" sts are not depicted in the chart, and should always be worked in the background color. Colors C7-C12 are considered the background colors, with the exception of Row 53 of the chart, where C2 is used as the background color for one row. All shaping will take place while working the pattern chart. M1L and M1R increases, and SSK and K2tog decreases will be placed on either side of the column of purled side "seams." Round numbers refer to the patterned rounds only. The hem rounds are not counted. Therefore, the first patterned round will be considered Rnd 1 of the sweater body. Keep track of your current chart rounds separately.

Setup Rnd – Pattern Rnd 1: Attach colors C10 and C4. Begin knitting pattern repeat from Row 1 of Chart at st designated for your size. *K131 (139, 147, 155, 163, 169, 177, 193, 207) in pattern, P1 in C10; rep from * once more across the back, beginning again at st designated for your size.

Knit in pattern for 5 (5, 5, 5, 6, 9, 9, 7, 10) more rnds.

Continue working around body in pattern as established, and begin working decreases in pattern as follows on next rnd, number 7 (7, 7, 7, 8, 11, 11, 9, 12).

Decrease Rnd: *SSK, work to two sts before side "seam," K2tog, P1, SM; rep from * once. 4 sts dec.

Decreases Continue to Waist: Continue knitting in pattern, working all rnds even, except rep Decrease Rnd on the following rnds:

Size 32.5: 13, 18, 23, 28, 32, 36, 40, 44, 48, 52. Dec to 220 sts.
Size 34: 13, 18, 23, 28, 33, 38, 42, 46, 50, 54. Dec to 236 sts.
Size 36.25: 13, 19, 24, 29, 34, 39, 43, 47, 51, 55. Dec to 252 sts.
Size 38.25: 13, 19, 24, 29, 34, 39, 44, 49, 53, 57. Dec to 268 sts.
Size 40.25: 14, 20, 25, 30, 35, 40, 45, 50, 55, 59. Dec to 284 sts.
Size 42.25: 20, 25, 30, 35, 40, 45, 50, 55, 60. Dec to 300 sts.
Size 43.75: 21, 27, 33, 39, 45, 51, 57, 62. Dec to 320 sts.
Size 48: 16, 22, 30, 38, 45, 52, 59, 66. Dec to 352 sts.
Size 52.25: 22, 30, 38, 46, 54, 62, 69. Dec to 384 sts.

Waist: Knit 16 rnds even for the waist. 68 (70, 71, 73, 75, 76, 78, 82, 85) rnds worked.

Begin working increases in pattern on the next Rnd as follows.
Increase Rnd: *M1L in pattern, work in pattern to side "seam," M1R in pattern, P1 in background color; rep from * once. 4 sts inc.

Increases Continue to Armhole: Continue knitting in pattern, working all rnds even, except rep Inc Rnd on the following rnds:
Size 32.5: 76, 83, 89, 96, 103, 110, 116. Inc to 252 sts.
Size 34: 79, 86, 94, 101, 109, 116. Inc to 264 sts.
Size 36.25 80, 87, 95, 103, 111, 118. Inc to 280 sts.
Size 38.25: 82, 89, 97, 105, 113, 120. Inc to 296 sts.
Size 40.25: 84, 91, 99, 106, 114, 121. Inc to 312 sts.
Size 42.25: 85, 92, 100, 108, 116, 123. Inc to 328 sts.
Size 43.75: 90, 101, 112, 123. Inc to 340 sts.
Size 48: 94, 105, 116, 127. Inc to 372 sts.
Size 52.25: 97, 108, 119, 130. Inc to 404 sts.

Knit 6 (7, 7, 7, 7, 7, 10, 10, 10) rnds even, finishing after working a total of 122 (123, 125, 127, 128, 130, 133, 137, 140) rnds.

Establish Armhole Steek

Rnd 1: Work in pattern across front of body until 6 (5, 5, 7, 8, 8, 7, 8, 10) sts remain before purled side "seam" at right underarm; BO 14 (12, 12, 16, 18, 18, 15, 18, 22) sts for right armhole. Continue in pattern until 6 (5, 5, 7, 8, 8, 7, 8, 10) sts remain before purled side "seam" at left underarm. BO 14 (12, 12, 16, 18, 18, 15, 18, 22) sts for left armhole.

From this point forward, pattern color changes should be worked in the center of the left underarm steek, as there will be fewer loose ends to weave in later. Continue to track current chart rnd as well as number of rnds from the beginning of body patterning just after the hem.

Rnd 2, Sizes 32.5, 34, 36.25, 38.25, 40.25 ONLY: Continue across the front to the last live st, PM. Use backward loops to CO 7 steek sts in alternating colors across armhole gap, PM. Join to the next live st of the back and continue to work across the sweater back in pattern from the chart until you reach the next BO st. PM and CO 7 steek sts using backward loop method in alternating colors. Using a marker of a different color, PM for new beginning of rnd. Join to next live st of sweater front. 224 (240, 256, 264, 276) body sts, not counting steek sts.

Rnd 2, Sizes 42.25, 43.75, 48, 52.25 ONLY: K1, SSK, work to 3 sts before BO sts, K2tog, K1, PM. Use backward loops to CO 7 steek sts in alternating colors across armhole gap, PM. Join to the next live st of the back. Resume following charted pattern for following instructions: K1, SSK, work to 3 sts before BO sts, K2tog, K1,

PM. Use backward loop method to CO 7 steek sts in alternating colors. Using a marker of a different color, PM for new beginning of rnd. Join to next live st of sweater front. 4 sts dec. 288 (306, 332, 356) body sts, not counting steek sts.

On subsequent rnds continue to work steek sts in a birds-eye pattern and sweater body in pattern from chart as established, SM before and after steek sts. Stitch counts will *not* include steek sts.

Size 32.5, 40.25 Only: Knit 1 rnd even.

Armhole Shaping Decrease: *K1, SSK, work to 3 sts before steek, K2tog, K1, SM, K steek sts, SM; rep from * once. 4 sts dec.
Next Rnd: Work an Armhole Shaping Decrease rnd. 220 (236, 252, 260, 272, 284, 302, 328, 352) sts.
Repeat Armhole Decrease Rnd every 3 (2, 2, 2, 2, 1, 1, 1, 1) rnds 2 (2, 8, 7, 10, 3, 9, 14, 17) more times, then every 4 (3, 3, 3, 0, 2, 2, 2, 2) rnds 3 (5, 1, 2, 0, 8, 6, 3, 2) times. Dec to 200 (208, 216, 224, 232, 240, 244, 260, 276) sts.
Knit even through rnd 158 (162, 165, 169, 173, 176, 179, 186, 194).

Neckline
Establish Front Neck Steek: K41 (43, 44, 46, 48, 50, 51, 54, 58), place 18 (18, 20, 20, 20, 20, 20, 22, 22) sts on scrap yarn or a st holder, PM, CO 7 steek sts in alternating colors across neck opening gap, PM, join to the next live st, K41 (43, 44, 46, 48, 50, 51, 54, 58), SM, K steek sts, SM, K100 (104, 108, 112, 116, 120, 122, 130, 138), SM, K steek sts, SM.

Double Decrease Rnd: Work in pattern to 4 sts before neck steek, K3tog, K1, SM, K steek sts in birds-eye pattern, SM, K1, SSSK, finish knitting rnd as established. 4 sts dec.
Work a Double Decrease Rnd a total of 2 (2, 1, 2, 2, 2, 2, 2, 4) times. 37 (39, 42, 42, 44, 46, 47, 50, 50) front sts each side of steek. 161 (165, 167, 172, 176, 179, 182, 189, 199) rnds worked.

Neckline Decrease Rnd: Work in pattern to 3 sts before steek, K2tog, K1, SM, K steek sts in birds-eye pattern, SM, K1, SSK, finish knitting rnd as established. 2 sts dec.
During the final rnd of this section, BO all armhole steek sts before continuing on to Shoulder Shaping.
Work a Neckline Decrease Rnd 6 (6, 7, 6, 6, 6, 6, 6, 4) times, then every 3 (2, 2, 3, 2, 2, 2, 2, 2) rnds 4 (3, 2, 3, 2, 1, 3, 4, 5) times, then every 0 (3, 3, 4, 3, 3, 3, 3, 3) rnds 0 (2, 3, 1, 3, 4, 3, 2, 1) times. Sizes 43.75, 48, 52.25: BO armhole steeks on final rnd. Front dec to 54 (56, 60, 64, 66, 70, 70, 76, 80) sts.
Work even for 4 (4, 3, 4, 1, 1, 0, 0, 0) rnds, binding off armhole steeks on final rnd. 183 (187, 190, 195, 196, 200, 203, 209, 216) rnds worked.

Front Shoulder Shaping
Front shoulder shaping will be worked flat, knitting across, then purling back in pattern. Chart rows are read on the RS from right to left, and WS from left to right. When finished, you will attach yarn to work the back shoulder and neck shaping separately. Continue to knit the body in pattern from the chart and the steek in birds-eye check. SM on either side of the steek as you come to them.

BO 5 (5, 5, 5, 4, 5, 4, 4, 4) sts at the beginning of next 6 (4, 10,

8, 4, 12, 10, 14, 18) rows, then BO 6 (6, 0, 6, 5, 0, 5, 5, 0) sts at the beginning of next 2 (4, 0, 1, 8, 0, 4, 2, 0) rows. BO remaining 6 (6, 5, 9, 5, 5, 5, 5, 4) sts.

Back Shoulder and Neck Shaping
Back shoulder shaping is worked flat, purling back in pattern as the front shaping was done.
Note: *The back neck shaping will begin during the shoulder shaping, so it is imperative that you read both sections before continuing.* Once the neck shaping begins, the right and left shoulders will be worked separately. The BOs take place at the *beginnings* of the rows, alternating between the neck opening and shoulder slope. Therefore, one shoulder will be one row longer than the other and require that you work an additional row even to compensate.
Turn garment to work on RS of back. Count 50 (52, 54, 56, 58, 60, 61, 65, 69) sts and PM at center of back. SM as you work each row to maintain center point until center neck sts are BO. Attach yarn to back right shoulder to continue in pattern.

Back Shoulder Shaping
At *each* shoulder at the beginning of rows, BO 5 (5, 5, 5, 4, 5, 4, 4, 4) sts 3 (2, 5, 4, 2, 6, 5, 7, 9) times, then 6 (6, 0, 6, 5, 0, 5, 5, 0) sts 1 (2, 0, 1, 4, 0, 2, 1, 0) times.
AT THE SAME TIME, work Back Neck Shaping: At row 184 (190, 194, 197, 201, 205, 209, 216, 225) BO center 18 (18, 20, 20, 20, 20, 20, 22, 22) sts –that's 9 (9, 10, 10, 10, 10, 10, 11, 11) sts BO on each side of the center marker. Remove marker. At *each* side of neck on the rows which *begin* at the neck side, BO 7 (8, 7, 10, 9, 9, 10, 10, 12) sts 2 (1, 2, 1, 1, 1, 1, 1, 1) times, then 0 (7, 0, 2, 3, 3, 3, 3, 3) sts 0 (1, 0, 2, 2, 2, 2, 2, 2) times.

Work even 1 row if necessary to finish with row 191 (195, 200, 204, 208, 212, 217, 225, 234). BO remainder of sts.

Sleeves (make 2 the same)
Bottom Folded Hem
Like the body, each sleeve begins with a folded St st hem. It is sewn up with thread during the finishing process. The sleeves are knit one at a time in the round until you reach the cap, which is knit flat. There is a faux P1 "seam" that runs up the underside.

With smaller needles, and C1, CO 56 (58, 60, 64, 66, 66, 68, 72, 76) sts. PM and join to work in the round, being careful not to twist sts.
Work in St st for 1.5".
Change to larger needles and purl 1 round for the Turning Ridge.
Knit the outside of the folded hem, establishing "seam" as follows: K to last st, P1. Rep this rnd until second side of hem measures 1.5".
Knit 12 (10, 10, 10, 9, 7, 7, 6, 5) more rnds even, then begin increases.

Increase Round: M1L, K to "seam" st, M1R, P1. 2 sts inc.
Work an Increase Rnd. Continue in St st, rep Inc Rnd every 12 (10, 10, 10, 9, 7, 7, 6, 5) rnds 6 (4, 14, 12, 14, 4, 11, 10, 10) more times, then every 13 (11, 0, 11, 10, 8, 8, 7, 6) rnds 5 (9, 0, 2, 2, 15, 9, 13, 17) more times. Inc to 80 (86, 90, 94, 100, 106, 110, 120, 132) sts.

Knit 7 (7, 8, 9, 8, 8, 7, 8, 8) rnds even. Sleeve should measure about 18 (18, 18.25, 18.5, 18.75, 18.75, 18.75, 19, 19)" from turning ridge of cuff.

Sleeve Cap

Begin working flat. Continue in St st, knitting the right side rows and purling the wrong side rows.

Sizes 32.5 & 34 Only: BO 6 (7) sts at beginning of next two rows. 68 (72) sts.

Sizes 36.25, 38.25, 40.25, 42.25, 43.75, 48, 52.25 Only:
Next Row (RS): BO 6 (7, 7, 8, 8, 7, 9) sts at beginning of next row.
Next Row (WS): BO 7 (8, 8, 9, 9, 8, 10) sts at the beginning of row, work to 3 sts before end of row, SSP, P1. 76 (78, 84, 88, 92, 104, 112) sts.

Sizes 36.25 & 38.25 Only: Work 1 row even.

All Sizes, Decrease Rounds

Use the following instructions for working decreases on the sleeve caps depending on whether you are working a RS row or a WS row:

If working a RS row: K1, SSK, work to 3 sts before end of row K2tog, K1. 2 sts dec.

If working a WS row: P1, P2tog, work to 3 sts before end of row, SSP, P1. 2 sts dec.

*Dec next rnd, then work 1 (1, 1, 1, 0, 0, 0, 0, 0) rnd even; rep from * 4 (3, 4, 4, 0, 0, 0, 3, 3) more times. 58 (64, 66, 68, 82, 86, 90, 96, 104) sts remain.

*Dec next rnd, then work 3 (2, 3, 3, 1, 1, 1, 1, 1) rnd even; rep from * 2 (0, 1, 1, 4, 4, 5, 3, 3) more times. 52 (62, 62, 64, 72, 76, 78, 88, 96) sts remain.

*Dec next rnd, then work 2 (3, 2, 2, 3, 2, 2, 2, 2) rnd even; rep from * 3 (3, 5, 5, 0, 8, 6, 7, 5) more times. 44 (54, 50, 52, 70, 58, 64, 72, 84) sts remain.

*Dec next rnd, then work 1 (2, 1, 1, 2, 1, 1, 1, 1) rnd even; rep from * 5 (2, 5, 5, 6, 4, 7, 4, 8) more times. 32 (48, 38, 40, 56, 48, 48, 62, 66) sts remain.

Size 32: BO remainder.

*Dec next rnd, then work 1 (0, 0, 1, 0, 0, 0, 0) rnd even; rep from * 5 (0, 0, 4, 2, 2, 6, 5) more times. 36 (36, 38, 46, 42, 42, 48, 54) sts remain.

Sizes 36.25, 38.25, 42.25, 43.75, 48, 52.25: BO remainder.

Size 34 & 40.25 Only: *Dec next rnd; rep from * 0 (2) more times. 34 (40) sts remain. BO remainder.

Finishing

Steeks: Turn sweater inside out. Reinforce steeks by hand stitching or machine stitching with a sharp needle and contrasting thread one st to either side of center st. Use very small sts that will stretch, such as hand backstitching or a small machine zig-zag. Take care to try to pierce the yarns with your sewing thread instead of slipping your needle between the yarns. With very sharp scissors, carefully cut through the center column of sts.

Block pieces to schematic measurements.

Neckband

Sew shoulder seams with yarn and a yarn needle. With C12 and larger circular needle, and RS facing, PU and K about 54 (54, 55, 57, 57, 58, 60, 64, 67) sts along back neck opening and 90 (91, 94,

95, 96, 99, 102, 106, 111) sts around front neck opening to conceal the steek. PM and join for working in rnd. K 4 rnds. Change to smaller needle, K 3 rnds. Purl 1 rnd for Turning Ridge. K 3 rnds. Change to larger needle, K 5 rnds. Loosely BO all sts. Fold edging along turning ridge and sew in place on the inside of garment with sharp sewing needle and matching thread.

Set sleeves into armholes, easing to fit, sew in. Fold cuff edgings and hem to inside of garment and sew in place with sharp sewing needle and matching thread. Whipstitch cut edges in place inside your garment, taking care that it does not show through to RS. Weave in ends or braid them down the inside side "seam."

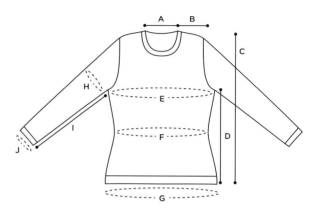

A 6 (6, 6.25, 6.25, 6.5, 6.5, 6.5 7, 7.5)"
B 3.5 (3.5, 3.75, 4.25, 4.25, 4.5, 4.5, 5, 5.25)"
C 24 (24.5, 25, 25.5, 26, 26.5, 27, 28, 29)"
D 15.75 (16, 16.25, 16.5, 16.5, 16.75, 17.25, 17.5, 18)"
E 32.25 (34, 36.25, 38.25, 40.25, 42.25, 43.75, 48, 52.25)"
F 28.5 (30.5, 32.5, 34.5, 36.75, 38.75, 41.25, 45.5, 49.5)"
G 34 (36.25, 38.25, 40.25, 42.25, 43.75, 46, 50, 53.75)"
H 10.25 (11, 11.5, 12.25, 13, 13.75, 14.25, 15.5, 17)"
I 18 (18, 18.25, 18.5, 18.75, 18.75, 18.75, 19, 19)"
J 7.25 (7.5, 7.75, 8.25, 8.5, 8.5, 8.75, 9.25, 9.75)"

Carivel Chart

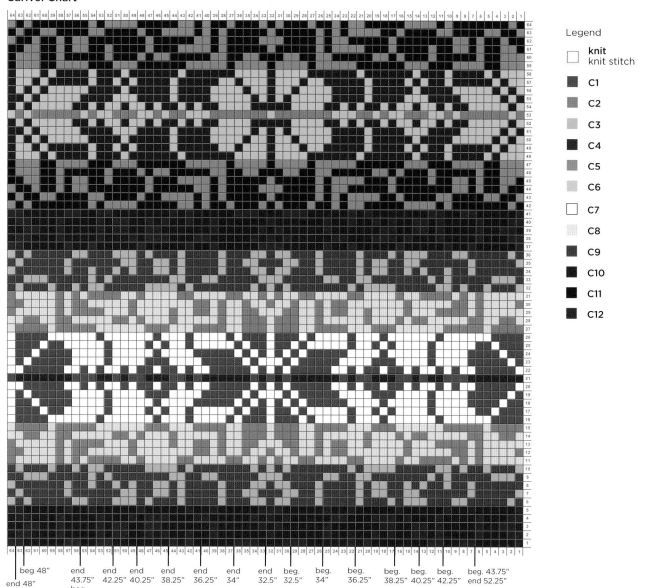

Legend

- ☐ **knit** — knit stitch
- ■ C1
- ■ C2
- ■ C3
- ■ C4
- ■ C5
- ■ C6
- ☐ C7
- ▦ C8
- ■ C9
- ■ C10
- ■ C11
- ■ C12

end 48" beg 48" end 43.75" beg 52.25" end 42.25" end 40.25" end 38.25" end 36.25" end 34" end 32.5" beg. 32.5" beg. 34" beg. 36.25" beg. 38.25" beg. 40.25" beg. 42.25" beg. 43.75" end 52.25"

BITTERLAKE CARDIGAN

by Allison Griffith

FINISHED MEASUREMENTS

27.75 (33, 38.75, 42.5, 46.5, 52, 55, 60.75)"
finished bust measurement; garment is
meant to be worn with little to no ease.

YARN

Knit Picks Wool of the Andes Sport (100%
Peruvian Highland Wool; 137 yards/50g):
MC Thirst Heather 25960 6 (7, 8, 10, 13, 15,
16, 18) balls, C1 Fedora 25272 3 (3, 3, 3, 4,
4, 4, 4) balls, C2 Bramble Heather 25278 1
ball all sizes, C3 Mink Heather 25275 1 ball
all sizes, C4 White 25269 1 ball all sizes,
C5 Saffron 25284 1 (1, 1, 2, 2, 2, 2) balls.

NEEDLES

Optional: US 5 (3.75mm) straight or
circular needles, or size to obtain gauge
US 5 (3.75mm) DPNs, or size to obtain
gauge

US 5 (3.75mm) 24" or longer circular
needle depending on size knit, or size to
obtain gauge

NOTIONS

Crochet Hook for provisional CO
Split-ring Stitch Markers or Safety Pins
Scrap Yarn for provisional cast on
Stitch Holder or Scrap Yarn
Stitch Markers
Yarn Needle
26 (26, 26, 26, 26, 28, 28, 28)" separating
plastic zipper in a coordinating color to C1
Sewing needle and thread in coordinating
color to C1

GAUGE

24 sts and 32 rows = 4" in St st, blocked.
1 repeat of Fair Isle Chart A= 2.5" square,
blocked.

Bitterlake Cardigan

Notes:

The Bitterlake Cardigan is a seamless sweater, knit from the neck down. A series of short rows at the back of the neck form the shoulders, then stitches are set aside for sleeves. The body is knit with optional waist shaping. Sleeves are then picked up and knit from reserved stitches. Once the main portion of the sweater is completed, the Fair Isle border is picked up and knit in the round on long circular needles, then the border facing is folded over and the live stitches are carefully sewn down to the inside of the sweater, hiding the wrong side of the colorwork and creating a smooth, professional finish. The sweater is then blocked lightly and a zipper is hand-sewn in.

Provisional Cast On (Crochet Chain method)

Using a crochet hook several sizes too big for the yarn, make a slipknot and chain for 1". Hold knitting needle in left hand. With yarn in back of the needle, work next chain st by pulling the yarn over the needle and through the chain st. Move yarn back to behind needle, and repeat for the number of sts required. Chain a few more sts off the needle, then break yarn and pull end through last chain. CO sts will be incorrectly mounted; knit into the back of these sts. To unravel (when sts need to be picked up), pull chain end out, and the chain should unravel, leaving live sts.

Increase Slant Right or Slant Left (used in shoulder shaping, optional waist shaping, and Chart B)

Increase Slant Right: Insert your right needle into the st below the next st on your left needle. Knit this st.

Increase Slant Left: Use your left needle to pick up the st that is two sts below the first st on your right needle. Knit this st.

Wrap and Turn (W&T)

Work until the stitch to be wrapped. If knitting: bring yarn to the front of the work, slip next st as if to purl, return the yarn to the back; turn work and slip wrapped st onto RH needle. Continue across row. If purling: bring yarn to the back of the work, slip next st as if to purl, return the yarn to the front; turn work and slip wrapped st onto RH needle. Continue across row.

Picking up wraps: Work to the wrapped st. If knitting, insert the RH needle under the wrap(s), then through the wrapped st K-wise. Knit the wrap(s) together with the wrapped st. If Purling, slip the wrapped st P-wise onto the RH needle, and use the LH needle to lift the wrap(s) and place them on the RH needle. Slip wrap(s) and unworked st back to LH needle; purl all together through the back loop.

S2KP2 Centered Double Decrease (Slip 2, Knit 1, Pass 2 Over)

Slip two sts together as if to knit, K one st, then pass the 2 slipped sts over the st you just knit. 2 sts dec.

DIRECTIONS

Shoulders

With MC, CO 58 (70, 82, 92, 102, 114, 124, 136) using a provisional CO. Prepare to work back and forth.

P 1 WS row.

(K2, inc 1 by knitting into the stitch below) across. 87 (105, 123, 138, 153, 171, 186, 204) sts.

On the next row, purl across and inc 1 (1, 1, 0, 1, 1, 0, 0) st. 88 (106, 124, 138, 154, 172, 186, 204) sts.

Short Rows

RS: K to 35 (42, 50, 55, 61, 68, 74, 82) before the end. W&T.

WS: P to 35 (42, 50, 55, 61, 68, 74, 82) before the end. W&T.

K to end of row, picking up and knitting wrap when you come to it.

P 1 row, picking up and purling wrap when you come to it.

K to 27 (32, 37, 41, 46, 52, 55, 61) before the end. W&T.

P to 27 (32, 37, 41, 46, 52, 55, 61) before the end. W&T.

K to end of row, picking up and knitting wrap when you come to it.

P 1 row, picking up and purling wrap when you come to it.

K to 18 (20, 25, 28, 30, 34, 37, 40) before the end. W&T.

P to 18 (20, 25, 28, 30, 34, 37, 40) before the end. W&T.

K to end of row, picking up and knitting wrap when you come to it.

P 1 row, picking up and purling wrap when you come to it.

Work even in St st (K on RS, P on WS) until piece measures 2 (2, 2, 2, 2, 2, 2.25, 2.25)" from CO along front edge. End with a WS row.

On the next row, (K2, inc 1) across. 132 (159, 186, 207, 231, 258, 279, 306) sts.

Work even in St st until piece measures 3.5 (3.5, 4, 4.25, 4.5, 4.75, 5, 5.25)" from CO along front edge. End with a WS row.

On the next row, (K3, inc 1) across. 176 (212, 248, 276, 308, 344, 372, 408) sts.

Work even in St st until piece measures 5.5 (5.5, 6.25, 6.5, 7, 7.5, 7.75, 8)" from CO along front edge. End with a WS row.

On the next row, (K4, inc 1) across. 220 (265, 310, 345, 385, 430, 465, 510) sts.

Work even in St st until piece measures 8 (8, 9, 9.5, 10, 10.5, 11, 11.5)" from CO along front edge. End with a WS row.

Divide for Body and Sleeves

Next Row (RS): K 23 (31, 39, 43, 49, 57, 60, 69) sts for Left Front, place 50 (58, 66, 74, 82, 90, 98, 106) sts onto scrap yarn or stitch holders for Left Sleeve, using a Provisional CO, CO 8 (10, 12, 14, 14, 16, 16, 18) sts for Left Underarm, K 74 (87, 100, 111, 123, 136, 149, 160) sts for Back, place 50 (58, 66, 74, 82, 90, 98, 106) sts onto scrap yarn or stitch holders for Right Sleeve, using a Provisional CO, CO 8 (10, 12, 14, 14, 16, 16, 18) sts for Right Underarm, K 23 (31, 39, 43, 49, 57, 60, 69) sts for Right Front. 136 (169, 202, 225, 249, 282, 301, 334) sts.

Body

Optional Waist Shaping

Next Row (WS): P 27 (36, 45, 50, 56, 65, 68, 78), PM, P 82 (97, 112, 125, 137, 152, 165, 178), PM, P to end.

Work even, continuing St st until piece measures 2" from underarms. Work Decrease Row as follows:

Decrease Row: *K to 2 sts before M, SSK, SM, K2tog; rep from *, K to end. 4 sts dec.

Work until piece measures 4.25 (4.25, 4, 3.75, 3.75, 4, 4, 4)" from underarms. Work Decrease Row.

Work until piece measures 6.75 (6.75, 6.25, 6, 5.75, 6.5, 6.25, 6.25)" from underarms. Work Decrease Row.

Work until piece measures 9.25 (9.25, 8.75, 8.5, 8.25, 9.5, 9.25, 8.75)" from underarms. Work Increase Row as follows:

Increase Row: *K to M, inc 1 (slant left), SM, inc 1 (slant right) repeat from *, K to end.

Work until piece measures 11.75 (11.75, 11, 10.75, 10.25, 12, 11.5, 11)" from underarms. Work Increase Row.

Work until piece measures 14 (14, 13, 12.5, 12, 14, 13.5, 13)" from underarms. Work Increase Row.

All Sizes

Work even in St st until piece measures 14.5 (14.5, 13.5, 13, 12.5, 14.5, 14, 13.5)" from underarms, ending with a WS row. Sweater should measure 22.5 (22.5, 22.5, 22.5, 22.5, 25, 25, 25)" from neck along front edge.

For size 27.75 only:

K, inc 5 sts evenly across the row.

For all other sizes:

K, decreasing (0, 5, 14, 10, 15, 6, 11) sts evenly across the row. Transfer the remaining 141 (169, 197, 211, 239, 267, 295, 323) sts to scrap yarn or stitch holders and proceed to Sleeves.

Sleeves (work 2 the same)

Transfer 50 (58, 66, 74, 82, 90, 98, 106) sleeve sts from scrap yarn to DPNs. Then, remove the provisional CO at the underarm, transfer the first 4 (5, 6, 7, 7, 8, 8, 9) sts, PM, transfer the remaining 4 (5, 6, 7, 7, 8, 8, 9) sts. 58 (68, 78, 88, 96, 106, 114, 124) sts.

Beginning at the M, knit sleeve in St st with MC in the rnd (K every rnd) until it measures 4.5 (4, 4, 3.5, 3.25, 3, 3.25, 1.5)" from underarm. Work Decrease Round as follows.

Decrease Round: K2tog, K to 2 sts before M, SSK, SM. 2 sts dec. Continue to knit in the round, working a Decrease Round every 12 (8, 10, 8, 10, 8, 9, 8)th rnd 6 (10, 8, 11, 9, 12, 11, 14) total times. 46 (48, 62, 66, 78, 82, 92, 96) sts. End with a Decrease Round.

Continue in St st, until the sleeve measures 14.5 (15, 15, 15.5, 15.5, 16, 16.5, 16.5)" from underarm. For longer or shorter sleeves, add or omit rows here.

On the next round, decrease 4 (6, 6, 10, 8, 12, 8, 12) sts evenly across the round. 42 (42, 56, 56, 70, 70, 84, 84) sts. Break yarn.

Cuff

Join C1 and K 2 rnds.
Work Chart A 3 (3, 4, 4, 5, 5, 6, 6) times around the cuff, breaking and joining colors as indicated by the chart. Work all 13 chart rows.

Cuff Facing

Continue with only C1, K 2 rounds.
P 1 rnd.
(K12, K2tog) around. 39 (39, 52, 52, 65, 65, 78, 78) sts.
K 19 rnds.
Break yarn, leaving a very long tail. Weave in all colorwork ends, being careful not to disrupt the Fair Isle pattern. Then, fold Cuff

Facing to the inside of the sleeve, hiding the WS of the colorwork. With the long tail and a tapestry needle, carefully sew live sts into the purl bumps of the first row of C1, being careful to keep your sts invisible on the RS of the sleeve.

Fair Isle Border

With your longest circular needle, pick up sts around the edge of the sweater as follows:

Remove the provisional CO from the Neck and transfer the 58 (70, 82, 92, 102, 114, 124, 136) sts to your needle.

With RS facing, sl 29 (41, 53, 49, 59, 57, 67, 79) sts from the left to the right needle, PM. This is the beginning of the rnd.

With C1, K the remaining 29 (29, 29, 43, 43, 57, 57, 57) Neck sts.

PU 1 st in the corner. Mark this st with a split-ring stitch marker or a safety pin.

PU 127 (127, 127, 127, 127, 141, 141, 141) sts along Left Front.

PU 1 st in the corner. Mark this st with a split-ring stitch marker or a safety pin.

Knit the reserved 141 (169, 197, 211, 239, 267, 295, 323) bottom Body sts.

PU 1 st in the corner. Mark this st with a split-ring stitch marker or a safety pin.

PU 127 (127, 127, 127, 127, 141, 141, 141) sts along Right Front.

PU 1 st in the corner. Mark this st with a split-ring stitch marker or a safety pin.

Knit the remaining 29 (41, 53, 49, 59, 57, 67, 79) sts from the Neck. You will have 457 (497, 537, 561, 599, 667, 705, 745) sts total.

Working in the rnd, K to 2 sts before end of rnd M, K2tog, SM.

Then, work all rnds of charts as follows, making sure that the marked corner sts line up with the center sts of Chart B. Break and join colors as indicated by the charts.

Work Chart A 2 (2, 2, 3, 3, 4, 4, 4) times (Neck).
Work Chart B once, working increases as indicated.
Work Chart A 9 (9, 9, 9, 9, 10, 10, 10) times (Left Front).
Work Chart B once, working increases as indicated.
Work Chart A 10 (12, 14, 15, 17, 19, 21, 23) times (Bottom).
Work Chart B once, working increases as indicated.
Work Chart A 9 (9, 9, 9, 9, 10, 10, 10) times (Right Front).
Work Chart B once, working increases as indicated.
Work Chart A 2 (2, 2, 3, 3, 4, 4, 4) times (Neck).
Work Chart C for your size one time. For sizes 27.75 and 52, omit Chart C.

Fair Isle Border Facing

Continue with only C1, K 1 rnd, working increases at corners as established.
K 1 rnd.
P 1 rnd.
K 1 rnd.
*Work 2 Decrease Rounds as follows:

Decrease Round: (K to 1 st before marked corner st, S2KP2, centering decrease over the corner st) four times, K to end. 8 sts dec.
K 1 rnd.
Repeat from * 5 more times (12 rounds total).
Work 1 more Decrease Round. 456 (496, 536, 560, 598, 666, 704, 744) sts.

Break yarn, leaving a very long tail. Weave in all colorwork ends, being careful not to disrupt the Fair Isle pattern. Then, fold Fair Isle Border Facing to the inside of the garment, hiding the WS of the colorwork. With the long tail and a yarn needle, carefully sew live sts into the purl bumps of the first row of C1, being careful to keep your sts invisible on the RS. When you run out of tail yarn, weave in end and continue sewing with another length of C1.

Finishing

Weave in any remaining ends.

Block to measurements, making sure to match the Left and Right Front colorwork as precisely as possible.

Once blocked, carefully sew the zipper to the Fair Isle Border with a sewing needle and matching thread. Start sewing .5" from the bottom and work toward the collar. Be careful to avoid puckering, and be sure to keep your sts as hidden as possible from the RS of the sweater.

Chart A

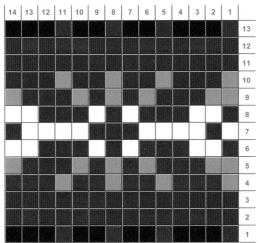

Chart B

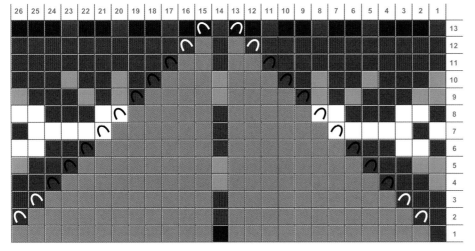

Legend

	knit
☐	knit stitch

	no stitch
	Placeholder - No stitch made.

	increase slant left
↶	Use your left needle to pick up the st that is two sts below the first st on your right needle. Knit this stitch.

	increase slant right
↷	Insert your right needle into the st below the next st on your left needle. Knit this stitch.

■	C1
■	C2
■	C3
☐	C4
■	C5

Chart C size 33

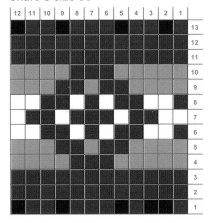

Chart C size 38.75

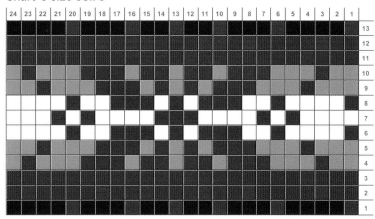

Chart C size 42.5

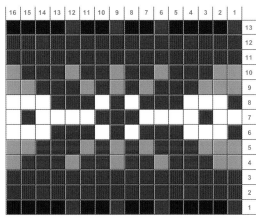

Chart C size 46.5

Chart C size 55

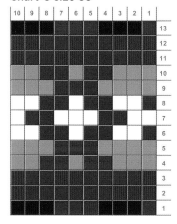

Chart C size 60.75

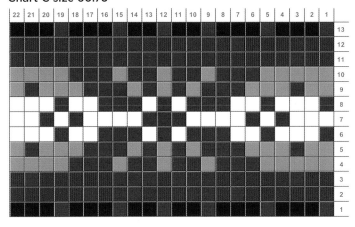

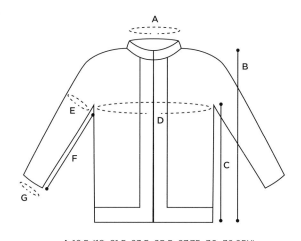

A 16.5 (19, 21.5, 23.5, 25.5, 27.75, 30, 32.25)″
B 27.5 (27.5, 27.5, 27.5, 27.5, 30, 30, 30)″
C 17 (17, 16, 15.5, 15, 17, 16.5, 16)″
D 27.75 (33, 38.75, 42.5, 46.5, 52, 55, 60.75)″
E 9.75 (11.25, 13, 14.75, 16, 17.75, 19, 20.75)″
F 17 (17.5, 17.5, 18, 18, 18.5, 19, 19)″
G 7.5 (7.5, 10, 10, 12.5, 12.5, 15, 15)″

CASSIA HAT AND MITTS

by Amy Mercer

FINISHED MEASUREMENTS

Hat: 21" circumference x 7.75" high
Mitts: 7" circumference x 8" high

YARN

Knit Picks Palette (100% Peruvian Highland Wool; 231 yards/50g): MC Regal 25089, 2 balls; C1 Turmeric 24251, 1 ball

NEEDLES

US 1 (2.25mm) DPNs or 32" or longer circular needle for Magic Loop technique, or size to obtain gauge

NOTIONS

Yarn Needle
Stitch Markers
Scrap Yarn

GAUGE

32 sts and 44 rows = 4" in stranded St st in the round, blocked.

Cassia Hat and Mitts

Notes:

The Cassia set includes a fitted beanie hat and fingerless mitts that combine an intricate stranded pattern with rich, modern jewel tones giving the set a fresh feeling. Knitted in the round, the Cassia Hat is a written and charted design with a garter stitch ribbed brim. The Cassia Mitts also have a charted pattern with written instructions that include a thick garter ribbed cuff to keep out the cold. Because both the hat and the mitts will be worked in the round, all charts are to be read and worked from right to left for all rows.

A special note about yarn dominance: If you are working your stranded knitting two-handed, the "foreground" yarn will be held in your left hand. If you are working with both yarns in one hand, the "foreground" yarn will be taken from below. The pattern instructions indicate which color is considered the "foreground" color for the particular row you are working.

Garter Ribbing (in the round over any number of sts)
Rnd 1: (K2, P2) to end.
Rnd 2: Knit.
Rep Rnds 1-2 for pattern.

Make 1 Left (M1L): Pick up the bar between the st you knit and the one you're about to knit, bringing the needle from front to back. Then knit into the back of the st.

Make 1 Right (M1R): Pick up the bar between the last st you knit and the one you're about to knit, bringing the needle from the back to the front. Then knit into the front of this st.

DIRECTIONS

Hat

With MC, CO 168 sts using your preferred method. PM and join to work in the round, being careful not to twist the sts.
Work Garter Ribbing 10 times for a total of 20 rows of ribbing.

Begin working the Cassia Hat Chart.
The chart will be repeated 7 times across the rnd. On Row 9, begin working stranded knitting with C1. For Rows 9 through 12, the C1 will be held as the "foreground" color.
On Row 14, switch your yarn dominance, so now the MC will be held as the "foreground" color.
On Row 36, switch your yarn dominance, so now the C1 will be held as the "foreground" color.
Continue working the Cassia Hat Chart through Row 44.

Crown Decreases

On Row 45 of the Cassia Hat Chart, you will begin decreasing for the crown of the hat. After completing the chart, break the yarn and thread tail through the remaining 14 sts to close up the top of the hat.

Finishing

Weave in ends with a yarn needle, wash and block to the measurements given in the diagram.

Mitts (make 2 the same)

With MC, CO 56 sts using your preferred method. PM and join to work in the round, being careful not to twist the sts.
Work Garter Ribbing 15 times for a total of 30 rnds of ribbing.

Begin working the Cassia Mitts Chart.
On Row 3, begin increases for the thumb gusset using the color indicated in the chart. If needed, PM before and after the increases to indicate the thumb gusset sts.
On Row 9 begin working stranded knitting with C1. For Rows 9 through 12, C1 will be held as the "foreground" color.
On Row 14, switch your yarn dominance, so now MC will be held as the "foreground" color.
Work the thumb gusset increases as indicated in the Cassia Mitts Chart through Row 25, until there are 23 thumb sts. On Row 26, place thumb gusset sts on scrap yarn and join the remaining 57 sts in the round. Continue working the Cassia Mitts Chart.
On Row 36, switch your yarn dominance, so now C1 will be held as the "foreground" color.
Continue working the Cassia Mitts Chart through Row 47.
Work Garter Ribbing for a total of 11 rnds, ending on Row 1 of the pattern.
Bind off.

Thumb

Put the 23 sts from scrap yarn back on the needles. With MC, starting from mitt edge K across the 23 sts and PU one extra st from the side of the mitt. 24 sts.
Join to work in the round, PM.
Work Garter Ribbing for a total of 7 rnds, ending on Row 1 of the pattern.
Bind off.

Finishing

Weave in ends with a yarn needle, wash and block to the measurements given in the diagram.

Hat Chart

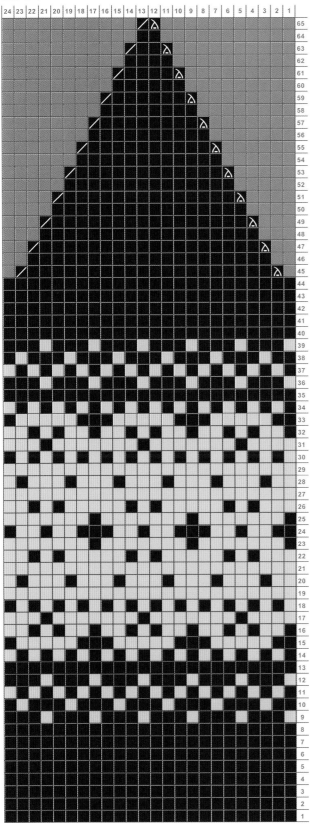

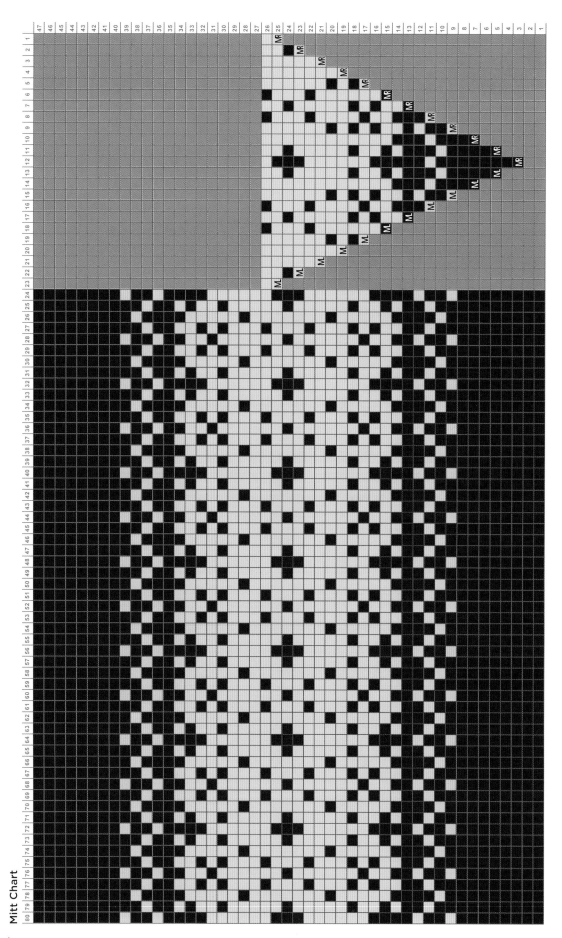

Mitt Chart

STYLIZED SWEATER

by Katy Banks

 For pattern support, contact KatyBanksDesigns@gmail.com

FINISHED MEASUREMENTS

To fit a bust measurement of 30 (34, 38, 42, 46, 50)". The finished hip measurement is 34.25 (36.25, 40, 44.25, 48, 52.75)"; choose the size which is closest to hip measurement at widest point, the garment will not fall this low so there will be positive ease at the hem.

YARN

Knit Picks Palette (100% Peruvian Highland Wool; 231 yards/50g): MC Stellar Heather 26053, 6 (6, 7, 7, 8, 8) balls; C1 Opal Heather 25096, C2 Raspberry Heather 24247, and C3 Oyster Heather 24559, 1 ball each

NEEDLES

US 5 (3.75mm) two 24" or longer circular needles and a spare DPN, or size to obtain gauge.
US 2 (2.75mm) 24" circular needles and DPNs or an additional 24" circular needle for two circulars technique, or size to obtain gauge.

NOTIONS

Yarn Needle
Scrap Yarn or Stitch Holder
Stitch Markers

GAUGE

23 sts and 34 rows = 4" on larger needles, in St st, blocked.
30 sts and 30 rows = 4" on smaller needles, in stranded St st in the round, blocked.

Stylized Sweater

Notes:

This pullover begins with the turned hem, worked in the round. The front and back continue from the hem separately and are worked back and forth through dolman sleeve shaping and shoulder short-row shaping. After seaming the sides and using a 3-needle bind-off technique for the shoulders and sleeves, cuffs are picked up and worked down in the round. A minimal turned neckband is picked up and worked last. The numbers in this pattern are always formatted the same way; for example, the number to be used for size 38 is always the second number inside parenthesis. Wherever the directions are for certain sizes only, this formatting remains the same and a "-" is used as a place holder for the sizes not included in those directions. Read each chart row from right to left, repeating the chart row across the round.

Stockinette Stitch with Garter Selvedges (worked flat over any number of sts)
Row 1 (RS): K.
Row 2 (WS): K1, P to the last st, K1.
Repeat Rows 1-2 for pattern.

DIRECTIONS

Hem

Begin with the facing; with smaller needles and MC, CO 256 (272, 300, 332, 360, 396) sts and join for working in the round being careful not to twist sts. PM and K every rnd until piece measures about 1 rnd less than 5". Do not cut MC. Change to C1 and P 1 rnd. Begin working Stylized Hem Chart. To avoid a jog in the colorwork pattern, slip the first st of every rnd P-wise WYIB and relocate M to the other side of the slipped st. Effectively, you are moving the M one st to the left every rnd; the chart has a colored line zigzagging along to illustrate the location of M.

Back

After completing Stylized Hem Chart, break all yarn colors. Place the first 128 (136, 150, 166, 180, 198) sts on scrap yarn or holder. Join MC and, with larger needle, CO 1 selvedge st, K 9 (9, 12, 8, 11, 12), *K2tog, K2; rep from * a total of 27 (29, 31, 37, 39, 43) times, K2tog, K 9 (9, 12, 8, 11, 12), CO 1 selvedge st. 102 (108, 120, 130, 142, 156) sts on needles. From this point on, you will be working back and forth in Stockinette Stitch with Garter Selvedges. Work 1 WS row.
Body Increase Row (RS): K3, M1, K to the last 3 sts, M1, K3. 2 sts inc. Work 3 (3, 3, 3, 5, 7) rows even. Repeat the last 4 (4, 4, 4, 6, 8) rows 20 (21, 22, 21, 9, 6) times more.
Sizes 30, 34, 46, and 50 only: Work Body Increase Row, then work 1 (1, -, -, 3, 3) rows even. Repeat the last 2 (2, -,- 4, 4) rows 3 (2, -, -, 5, 4) times more. 152 (158, 166, 174, 174, 180) sts on needles.
Continue for all sizes: At the end of the next 2 rows, CO 23 (24, 24, 25, 25, 26) sleeve sts. 198 (206, 214, 224, 224, 232) sts on needles. Work 34 (36, 38, 42, 50, 58) rows even.

Short Row Shaping

Shape shoulders as follows.
Back Short Row 1 (RS): K to 8 sts before end (before M after 1st time), W&T, PM.

Back Short Row 2 (WS): P to 8 sts before end (before M after 1st time), W&T, PM.
Repeat the last 2 rows 8 (4, 6, 3, 3, 6) times more.
Sizes 34, 38, 42, 46, and 50 only:
Back Short Row 3: K to 7 sts before M, W&T, PM.
Back Short Row 4: P to 7 sts before M, W&T, PM.
Repeat the last 2 rows - (4, 2, 6, 6, 3) times more.
Continue for all sizes: Work 2 rows even, removing M and working wraps together with the sts they are wrapping as you come to them. Place all sts on scrap yarn or stitch holder(s).

Front

Return the held hem sts to larger needle and work as for Back up to the Short Row Shaping. Sizes 34, 38, 42, 46, and 50 only: Work the first - (2, 2, 4, 4, 4) short rows as for Back. Continue for all sizes: shape shoulders and front neck as follows.
Directions are given to work both sides simultaneously, each with its own ball of yarn.
Front Short Row 1 (RS): K 89 (92, 95, 99, 99, 102), join second ball of MC and use it to BO 20 (22, 24, 26, 26, 28) center front sts, K to 8 (8, 8, 7, 7, 8) sts before end, W&T, PM.
Front Short Row 2 (WS): P to neck edge of right side; on left side, BO 6 (6, 7, 7, 7, 7) sts at neck edge, P to 8 (8, 8, 7, 7, 8) sts before end, W&T, PM.
Front Short Row 3: K to neck edge of left side; on right side, BO 6 (6, 7, 7, 7, 7) sts at neck edge, K to 8 (8, 8, 7, 7, 8) sts before M, W&T, PM.
Front Short Row 4: P to neck edge of right side; on left side, P to 8 (8, 8, 7, 7, 8) sts before M, W&T, PM.
Front Short Row 5: K to 3 sts before neck edge of left side, K2tog, K1; on right side, K1, SSK, K to 8 (8, 8, 7, 7, 8) sts before M, W&T, PM.
Front Short Row 6: Same as Row 4.
Repeat the last 2 rows 4 (1, 3, 4, 4, 2) times more.
Sizes 34, 38, and 50 only:
Front Short Row 7: K to 3 sts before neck edge of left side, K2tog, K1; on right side, K1, SSK, K to 7 sts before M, W&T, PM.
Front Short Row 8: P to neck edge of right side; on left side, P to 7 sts before M, W&T, PM.
Repeat the last 2 rows - (2, 0, -, -, 1) times more.
Continue for all sizes: 78 (81, 83, 87, 87, 90) sts on each side.
Front Short Row 9: K to neck edge of left side; on right side, K to 8 (7, 7, 7, 7, 7) sts before M, W&T, PM.
Front Short Row 10: P to neck edge of right side; on left side, P to 8 (7, 7, 7, 7, 7) sts before M, W&T, PM.
Repeat the last 2 rows once more. Work 2 rows even, removing M and working wraps together with the sts they are wrapping as you come to them.

Joining Back to Front and Working Neckband

Return the held Back sts to second larger needle. Hold the Front and Back with RS together. Begin at one cuff edge, using spare DPN to perform 3-Needle BO of one sleeve. Continue working across the back of the neck, BO 42 (44, 48, 50, 50, 52) sts. Continue with 3-Needle BO to the cuff of the second sleeve. Sew side seams.
With larger needles and MC, begin at the right shoulder seam. PU and K around neck opening, picking up one st for each BO st and

about 4 sts for every 5 rows along front neck vertical edges. K 2 rnds, P 1 rnd, K 2 rnds, BO all sts.

Cuffs

With smaller needles (DPNs, if you prefer) and MC, begin at the side seam of one sleeve opening and PU and K 64 (68, 76, 84, 92, 108) sts around the opening. PM to denote beginning of rnd. Work Stylized Cuff Chart using the same technique as described in the Hem section to avoid a jog in the colorwork pattern. Continuing with C1, P one rnd. Work cuff facing in MC until it meets the cuff CO rnd when folded along the purled turning rnd. Repeat for the other Cuff.

Finishing

Weave in ends, wash and block to diagram. Note that the diagram shows the garment after the facings are sewn in place; measure lengths to the purled turning rnds, not including the facings. After blocking is finished, turn the facings to the inside of the garment and sew in place.

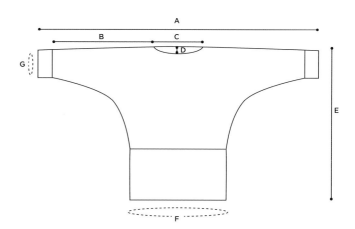

A 41 (42.5, 44, 45.5, 45.5, 47)"
B 13.5 (14, 14.5, 15.25, 15.25, 15.75)"
C 7.25 (7.75, 8.25, 8.75, 8.75, 9)"
D 2.25"
E 23.25 (24.25, 24.5, 25, 25.25, 25.25)"
F 34.25 (36.25, 40, 44.25, 48, 52.75)"
G 8.5 (9, 10.25, 11.25, 12.25, 14.5)"

Hem Chart

Legend

- **purl** — purl stitch
- **knit** — knit stitch
- MC
- C1
- C2
- C3

marker placement

Cuff Chart

DECO HAT

by Stephannie Tallent

FINISHED MEASUREMENTS
22" circumference x 8.75" high

YARN
Knit Picks Palette Bare (100% Peruvian Highland Wool; 462 yards/100g): A Natural 23851, 1 hank.
Knit Picks Palette (100% Peruvian Highland Wool; 231 yards/50g): B Bittersweet Heather 24239, C Lingonberry Heather 25998, D Raspberry Heather 24247, E Conch 24557; 1 ball each.

NEEDLES
US 2 (3mm) DPNs or two 24" circular needles for two circulars technique, or one 32" or longer circular needle for Magic Loop technique, or size to obtain gauge
US 1 (2.5mm) DPNs or two 24" circular needles for two circulars technique, or one 32" or longer circular needle for Magic Loop technique, or two sizes smaller than size to obtain gauge

NOTIONS
Yarn Needle
Stitch Markers (minimum 1 for beginning of round)

GAUGE
35.5 sts and 39 rows = 4" in stranded St st in the round on larger needles, blocked.

Deco Hat

Notes:

This hat is worked in the round from the brim up. The last stitch of the rounds prior to SK2P decrease rounds will be incorporated into the first SK2P of the decrease round; work the last stitch as charted, work the K2tog of the decrease, then pass the stitch over. This maintains the color pattern. Read each chart row from right to left.

DIRECTIONS
Brim

With smaller needles, CO 154 sts with Color B. PM and join in the round, being careful not to twist.

Purl 1 rnd.

Work (K1, P1) ribbing for 1.25".

Main Body of Hat

Change to larger needles.

Inc Rnd: *M1R, K4, M1R, K3, M1R, K4; rep from * to end. 196 sts.

Begin working chart, working repeat 7 times around. See notes above regarding decrease rounds.

Complete chart. Cut yarn, leave a 6" tail. Thread yarn through live sts and pull tightly to cinch hole closed.

Finishing

Weave in ends, wash and block.

Deco Chart

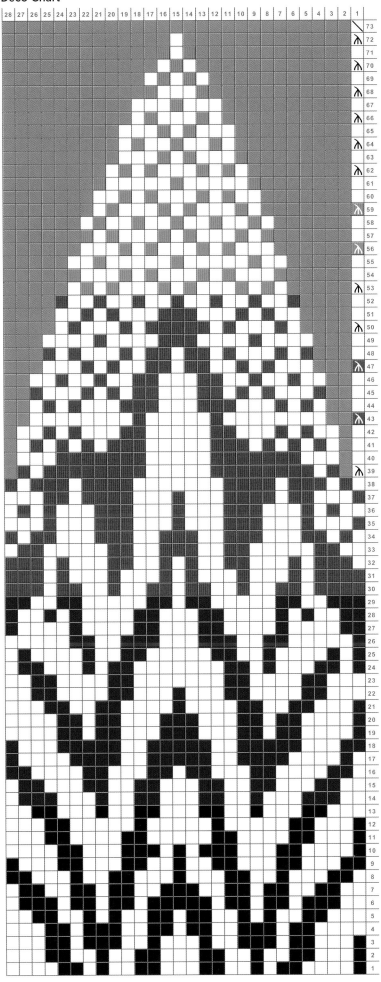

Legend

knit
knit stitch

sl1 k2tog psso
slip 1, k2tog, pass slip stitch over k2tog

No Stitch
Placeholder - No stitch made.

ssk
Slip one stitch as if to knit, slip another stitch as if to knit. Insert left-hand needle into front of these 2 stitches and knit them together

☐ A

■ B

■ C

■ D

■ E

FROST SLIPPERS

by Emily Kintigh

FINISHED MEASUREMENTS

9.5 (10, 10.5)" long

YARN

Knit Picks Wool of the Andes Worsted (100% Peruvian Highland Wool; 110 yards/50g): MC White 24065, 2 balls; C1 Hollyberry 23419, C2 Grizzly Heather 25641, 1 ball each.

NEEDLES

US 4 (3.5mm) 32" or longer circular needle for Magic Loop technique, or size to obtain gauge
US 3 (3.25mm) DPNs or two 24" circular needles for two circulars technique, or one 32" or longer circular needle for Magic Loop technique, or one size smaller than gauge needle

NOTIONS

Yarn Needle
9 Stitch Markers, 1 removable
Size D Crochet Hook

GAUGE

24 sts and 26 rows = 4" in stranded St st in the rnd on larger needles, blocked.

Frost Slippers

Notes:

The slippers tops are worked two at a time using the Magic Loop method with steeks between each slipper and where the cuff will be. The slipper bottoms are also worked two at a time with steeks between them.

Once the bottoms and tops are sewn together, stitches are picked up to work the cuff.

The charts are worked in the round, read each chart row from right to left.

To form the steeks, alternate working stitches in each color in the indicated sections on rounds with two colors.

Stockinette Stitch (St st, worked in the rnd)
All Rounds: K all sts.

2x2 Ribbing (in the round over a multiple of 4 sts)
All Rounds: (K2, P2) to end.

DIRECTIONS

Slipper Tops

The slippers are worked in the round from the heel to the toe.

With C2, (C1, C2) and larger needle, CO 4 (4, 4) steek sts, PM, CO 11 (12, 13) sts, PM, CO 8 (8, 8) steek sts, PM, CO 11 (12, 13) sts, PM, CO 8 (8, 8) steek sts, PM, CO 11 (12, 13) sts, PM, CO 8 (8, 8) steek sts, PM, CO 11 (12, 13) sts, PM, CO 4 (4, 4) steek sts. 76 (80, 84) sts. Place a removable st marker at the beginning of the round. This marker keeps track of the beginning of the rnd and is not counted as one of the markers indicated below. Join in the rnd using Magic Loop method, being careful not to twist sts.
Work the sts between the beginning of the rnd and the first marker, the second and third markers, the fourth and fifth markers, the sixth and seventh markers and the eighth marker and the end of the rnd as steeks.

Between the first and second marker, and the fifth and sixth marker, work the Small Right (Medium Right, Large Right) Chart. Between the third and fourth marker, and the seventh and eighth marker, work the Small Left (Medium Left, Large Left) Chart.
On the last rnd of all charts, BO the steek sts between the second and third markers, and the sixth and seventh markers, removing these markers. 60 (64, 68) sts.
Next Rnd: With C1, K to first section of bound off sts, CO 9 (11, 13) sts, continue knitting to second section of bound off sts, CO 9 (11, 13) sts, K to end. 78 (86, 94) sts.
Begin working Toe Chart between the first and second markers, and the third and fourth markers, while continuing to work steeks before the first marker, between the second and third markers, and after the last marker. At the end of the chart, BO all sts.

Soles

With C2 and larger needle, CO 4 (4, 4) steek sts, PM, CO 4 (6, 8) sts, PM, CO 8 (8, 8) steek sts, PM, CO 4 (6, 8) sts, PM, CO 4 (4, 4) steek sts. 24 (28, 32) sts. Place a removable st marker at the beginning of the round. This marker keeps track of the beginning of the rnd and is not counted as one of the markers indicated below. Join to work in the rnd using Magic Loop method, being careful not to twist sts.

Work the 4 sts before the first marker, the 8 sts between the second and third marker, and the 4 sts after the fourth marker, as steeks while following the directions below for the sections between the first and second markers, and the third and fourth markers. Work with C2 except where indicated to work with C1 according to the Sole Chart. Steek sts are not included in the instructions below, except in stitch counts.

Rnd 1: K to end.
Rnd 2: KFB, K to one st before M, KFB. 28 (32, 36) sts.
Rnd 3: K2, M1, K to 2 sts before M, M1, K2. 32 (36, 40) sts.
Rnd 4: K to end.
Rnd 5: K1, *M1, K 3 (4, 5) sts; work from * twice, M1, K1. 38 (42, 46) sts.
Rnd 6: Join C1 to steek, with C2, K3, work Rnd 1 of Sole Chart to 3 sts before M, K3.
Rnd 7: K1, M1, K1, work Rnd 1 of Sole Chart to 2 sts before M, K1, M1, K1. 42 (46, 50) sts.
Rnd 8: K3, work Rnd 2 of Sole Chart to 3 sts before M, K3.
Rnd 9: K1, M1, K1, work Rnd 2 of Sole Chart to 2 sts before M, K1, M1, K1. 46 (50, 54)
Rnd 10: K3, work Rnd 1 of Sole Chart to 3 sts before M, K3.
Rnd 11: Rep Rnd 7. 50 (54, 58) sts.
Rnd 12: K3, work Rnd 2 of Sole Chart to 3 sts before M, K3.
Rnd 13: K3, work Rnd 1 of Sole Chart to 3 sts before M, K3.

For 9.5" Size:
Rnds 14-20: Rep Rnds 12-13 three more times, then Rnd 12 once more.
Rnd 21: Rep Rnd 9. 54 sts.
Rnds 22-30: Rep Rnd 13, then Rnds 12-13 four more times.
Rnd 31: Rep Rnd 7. 58 sts.
Rnds 32-40: Rep Rnds 12-13 four more times, then Rnd 12 once more.
Rnd 41: Rep Rnd 9. 62 sts.
Rnds 42-50: Rep Rnd 13, then Rnds 12-13 four more times.
Move on to Toe Shaping.

For 10" Size:
Rnds 14-21: Rep Rnds 12-13.
Rnd 22: Rep Rnd 7. 58 sts.
Rnds 23-32: Rep Rnds 12-13.
Rnd 33: Rep Rnd 7. 62 sts.
Rnds 34-43: Rep Rnds 12-13.
Rnd 44: Rep Rnd 7. 66 sts.
Rnds 45-54: Rep Rnds 12-13.
Move on to Toe Shaping.

For 10.5" Size:
Rnds 14-22: Rep Rnds 12-13 four more times, then Rnd 12 once more.
Rnd 23: Rep Rnd 9. 62 sts.
Rnds 24-34: Rep Rnd 13, then Rnds 12-13 five more times.
Rnd 35: Rep Rnd 7. 66 sts.
Rnds 36-46: Rep Rnds 12-13 five more times, then Rnd 12 once more.
Rnd 47: Rep Rnd 9. 70 sts.
Rnds 48-58: Rep Rnd 13, then Rnds 12-13 five more times.
Move on to Toe Shaping.

Toe Shaping

Rnd 1: SSK, K1, work Rnd 2 of Sole Chart to 3 sts before M, K1, K2tog. 58 (62, 66) sts.

Rnd 2: K3, work Rnd 2 of Sole Chart to 3 sts before M, K3.

Rnd 3: SSK, K1, work Rnd 1 of Sole Chart to 3 sts before M, K1, K2tog. 54 (58, 62) sts.

Rnd 4: K3, work Rnd 1 of Sole Chart to 3 sts before M, K3.

Rnds 5-6: Rep Rnd 1. 46 (50, 54) sts.

Rnd 7: Cut C1 and work with C2 only. SSK, K to 2 sts before M, K2tog. 42 (46, 50) sts.

Rnds 8-10: Rep Rnd 7. 30 (34, 38) sts.

BO all sts.

Using crochet hook, reinforce the steeks down the middles of each steek section. There should be reinforced steeks along both sides of each slipper top, each foot opening as well as each slipper bottom.

Cut the steeks. Fold over and baste all steeks.

Block all pieces. Using mattress stitch seaming along the sides, and making invisible horizontal seams at the toe and back of the heel, sew the Sole to Slipper Top with wrong sides together and starting at the toe and working back towards the heel.

Sew the two sides of the CO edge of the Slipper Top together to form the back of the heel.

Repeat for second slipper.

Cuffs

With MC and smaller needles, PU 56 (60, 64) sts around the opening for the foot, PM for beginning of rnd. Work in 2x2 Ribbing until cuff measures 6" long, or desired length. For a cuff that does not fold over, work until the cuff measures 3" long.

Loosely BO all sts.

Repeat for second slipper.

Finishing

Weave in any remaining ends, and block again if desired.

Toe Chart

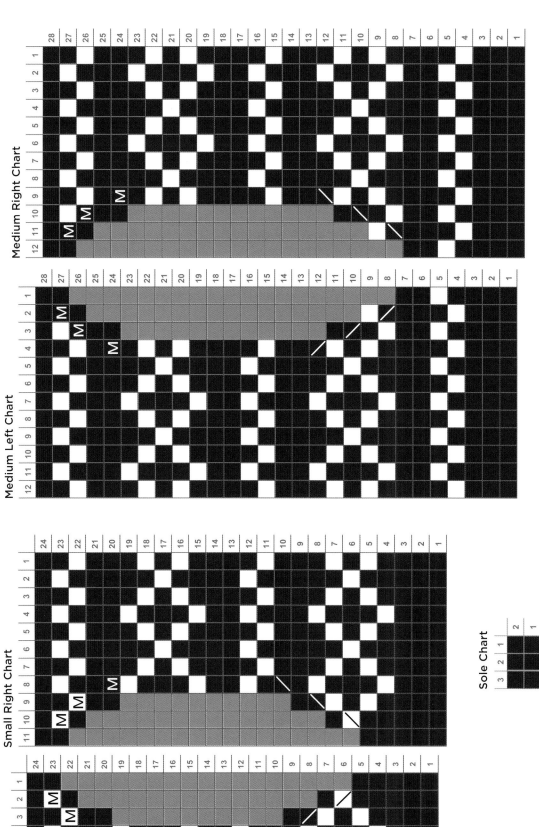

Medium Right Chart

Medium Left Chart

Small Right Chart

Small Left Chart

Sole Chart

Legend

knit
knit stitch

No Stitch
Placeholder - No stitch made.

ssk
Slip one stitch as if to knit, Slip another stitch as if to knit. Insert left-hand needle into front of these 2 stitches and knit them together

k2tog
Knit two stitches together as one

make one
Make one by lifting strand in between stitch just worked and the next stitch, knit into back of this thread.

M make one

MC

C1

C2

9.5" size. Work section outlined, working decreases shown in this color with yarn color indicated

10" size. Work section outlined, working decreases shown in this color with yarn color indicated

10.5" size. Work section outlined, working decreases shown in this color with yarn color indicated

pattern repeat

Large Right Chart

Large Left Chart

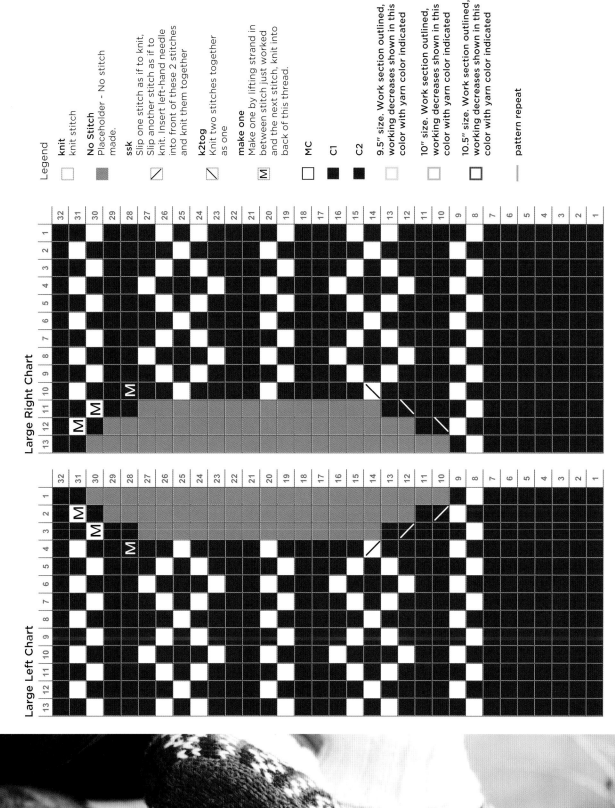

LAMIALES HAT AND COWL

by Zabet Kempfert

FINISHED MEASUREMENTS

Cowl: 24" circumference x 10" high
Hat: 18 (21)" circumference

YARN

Knit Picks Bare Palette (100% Peruvian
Highland Wool; 462 yards/100g): MC
Natural 23851, 1 hank.
Knit Picks Palette (100% Peruvian
Highland Wool; 231 yards/50g):
C1 Clematis Heather 24013, 1 ball; C2
Indigo Heather 26051, 1 ball; C3 Tidepool
Heather 24007, 1 ball; C4 Spruce 25535,
2 balls.

NEEDLES

US 3 (3.25mm) 16" or 24" circular needles,
or size to obtain gauge
DPNs in size needed to obtain gauge

NOTIONS

Yarn Needle
Stitch Markers

GAUGE

32 sts and 35 rows = 4" in stranded St st
in the round, blocked.

Lamiales Hat and Cowl

Notes:

The Lamiales Hat and Cowl feature corrugated ribbing, Latvian braids, and an intricate Fair Isle pattern against a colorful background. Knit with only 2 colors at a time, this set is a classic addition to your winter wardrobe.

Corrugated Ribbing

Round 1: (K2 in MC, K2 in C3) around.
Round 2: (P2 in MC, K2 in C3) around.
Repeat Rnd 2 to desired length.

Latvian Braid (Right-leaning)

Round 1: (K1 in MC, K1 in C4) around.
Round 2: Wyif, (P1 in MC, P1 in C4) around. When switching yarns, bring the yarn you are going to use for the next stitch under the yarn you just used.
Round 3: Wyif, (P1 in MC, P1 in C4) around. When switching yarns, bring the yarn you are going to use for the next stitch over the yarn you just used.

Latvian Braid (Left-leaning)

Round 1: (K1 in MC, K1 in C4) around.
Round 2: Wyif, (P1 in MC, P1 in C4) around. When switching yarns, bring the yarn you are going to use for the next stitch over the yarn you just used.
Round 3: Wyif, (P1 in MC, P1 in C4) around. When switching yarns, bring the yarn you are going to use for the next stitch under the yarn you just used.

Cowl
DIRECTIONS

Loosely CO 192 sts in MC. Pm and join to work in the round, being careful not to twist.

Join C3 and work in P2, K2 corrugated ribbing for 1.25". K one round in MC. Join C4 and work a right-leaning Latvian braid.

Begin working from Lamiales Chart, repeating the 24 st pattern 8 times around the cowl and reading each chart row from right to left. Work rounds 1-24 twice, then rounds 1-15 once.

With MC and C4, work a left-leaning Latvian braid. K one round in MC. With MC and C3, work in P2, K2 corrugated ribbing for 1.25".

Break CCs and loosely BO all sts in MC.

Hat
DIRECTIONS

Loosely CO 144 (168) sts in MC. Pm and join to work in the round, being careful not to twist.

Join C3 and work in P2, K2 corrugated ribbing for 1.25". K one round in MC. Join C4 and work a right-leaning Latvian braid.

Begin working from Lamiales Chart, repeating the 24 st pattern 6 (7) times around the hat and reading each chart row from right to left. Work rounds 1-24 once.

On the next round, begin working from Lamiales Decrease Chart, repeating the 24 st pattern 6 (7) times around the hat. Work rounds 1-29 once, following decreases as written. Switch to DPNs when necessary. After round 29 of Lamiales Decrease Chart, 24 (28) sts remain.

Break all yarns. Using C1, draw yarn end through remaining live sts. Draw tight to close hole. If desired, make a pompom with MC and attach to top of hat.

Finishing

Weave in ends, wash and block to finished measurements.

Decreases Chart

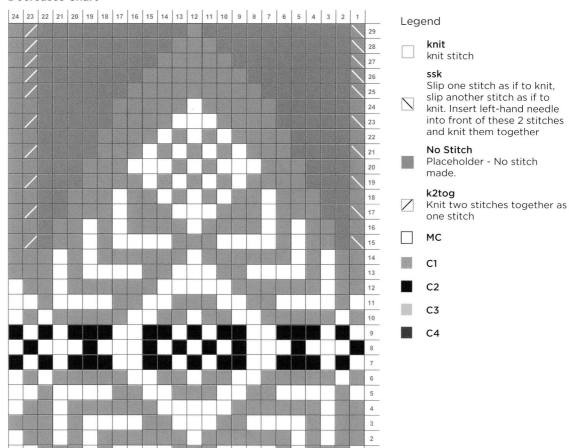

Legend

knit
knit stitch

ssk
Slip one stitch as if to knit, slip another stitch as if to knit. Insert left-hand needle into front of these 2 stitches and knit them together

No Stitch
Placeholder - No stitch made.

k2tog
Knit two stitches together as one stitch

☐ MC

▨ C1

■ C2

▨ C3

▨ C4

Lamiales Chart

FLOWER ISLAND CARDIGAN

by Gabrielle Vézina

 For pattern support, contact hello@gabriellevezina.com

FINISHED MEASUREMENTS

33.25 (34.75, 36.5, 39.5, 42.75, 46.75, 50.75)" finished bust measurement, buttoned; garment is meant to be worn with 0-2" of positive ease.

YARN

Knit Picks Bare Wool of the Andes Worsted (100% Peruvian Highland Wool; 220 yards/100g): MC Natural 23417, 4 (4, 4, 5, 5, 6, 6) skeins

Knit Picks Wool of the Andes Worsted (100% Peruvian Highland Wool; 110 yards/50g): C1 Pampas Heather 24074, 1 (1, 1, 2, 2, 2, 3) balls; C2 Bittersweet Heather 24652, 1 (1, 2, 2, 2, 2, 2) balls; C3 Forest Heather 23897, 1 ball.

NEEDLES

US 6 (4mm) 32" or longer circular needles plus optional DPN's for sleeves, or one size smaller than needle to obtain gauge

US 7 (4.5mm) 32" or longer circular needles plus optional DPN's for sleeves, or size to obtain gauge

NOTIONS

Yarn Needle
2 Stitch Markers, 2 Removable Stitch Markers
Scrap Yarn or Stitch Holder
Eight 7/8" Buttons

GAUGE

20 sts and 28 rows = 4" in St st on larger needles, blocked.

Flower Island Cardigan

Notes:

The Flower Island Cardigan is a seamless cardigan worked top-down. At the bottom of the body and sleeves, a flower pattern made of four colors makes this cardigan an original and gorgeous garment.

When working a chart flat, read RS rows (odd numbers) from right to left, and WS rows (even numbers) from left to right. Working in the round, read each chart row from right to left, as a RS row.

Wrap and Turn (W&T)

(RS) Bring yarn to front, sl one st, bring yarn to back, sl st back to LH needle, turn work.

(WS) Bring yarn to back, sl one st, bring yarn to front, sl st back to LH needle, turn work.

K1, P1 Ribbing (worked flat or in the rnd over an odd number of sts)

Row 1 (RS): *K1, P1; rep from * to last st, K1.
Row 2 (WS): P1, *K1, P1; rep from * to end of row.
Rep Rows 1-2 for pattern when working flat. To work in the rnd, rep Row 1 for every rnd.

DIRECTIONS

Body

Body is worked from the top down, starting with the back from shoulders to underarms, then stitches are picked up at the shoulders and both fronts are worked simultaneously, down to underarms. The two front pieces and back are then joined together, and the body is worked in one single piece from then.

Back

With larger needles, CO 65 (67, 69, 73, 77, 81, 87) sts. Place a removable M after 12 (12, 12, 12, 14, 14, 14) and 53 (55, 57, 61, 63, 67, 73) sts (to help identify sts to PU for front later). Work in St st (K on RS, P on WS) for 5.5 (5.5, 5.5, 6, 6, 6, 6.5)".

Shape Armholes

Use the M1 method to inc 1 st at each armhole edge every RS row 3 times, then every row 4 (5, 5, 6, 8, 10, 11) times. 79 (83, 85, 91, 99, 107, 115) sts.

Place sts on holder to work later for lower body and cut yarn.

Fronts

With RS facing and beginning at armhole edge, PU and K 12 (12, 12, 12, 14, 14, 14) sts from CO sts for right front, ending at first marker. With RS still facing, attach another ball of yarn at second marker, PU and K 12 (12, 12, 12, 14, 14, 14) sts from CO sts for left front, ending at armhole edge. Working each set of front sts separately, work in St st as for back for 4.25 (4.5, 4.5, 4.75, 5, 5, 5)". CO 5 (5, 5, 6, 6, 6, 7) sts at each neck edge every RS row 4 (3, 2, 4, 4, 2, 3) times, then CO 0 (6, 6, 0, 0, 7, 8) sts at each neck edge every RS row 0 (1, 2, 0, 0, 2, 1) times. At the same time, when piece measures 5.5 (5.5, 5.5, 6, 6, 6, 6.5)" (same length as back to beginning of armhole shaping), shape armholes as for back. 39 (41, 42, 45, 49, 53, 57) sts for each front.

Lower Body

Arrange sts on a long circular needle the following way: 39 (41, 42, 45, 49, 53, 57) sts from left front, 79 (83, 85, 91, 99, 107, 115) sts from back, 39 (41, 42, 45, 49, 53, 57) sts from right front.

Joining Row (RS): K39 (41, 42, 45, 49, 53, 57) sts from left front, CO 1 (1, 2, 3, 3, 4, 5) sts, PM, CO 1 (1, 2, 3, 3, 4, 5) sts, K79 (83, 85, 91, 99, 107, 115) sts from back, CO 1 (1, 2, 3, 3, 4, 5) sts, PM, CO 1 (1, 2, 3, 3, 4, 5) sts, K39 (41, 42, 45, 49, 53, 57) sts from right front. 161 (169, 177, 193, 209, 229, 249) sts.

Waist Shaping: Work even until work measures approximately 3 (3, 3.25, 3.25, 3.25, 3.5, 3.5)" from joining row. Starting on next row, dec 4 sts as follows; 1 st before and after each M, then rep every 1.5" two more times. 149 (157, 165, 181, 197, 217, 237) sts. Work even for 1.5". Inc 4 sts per row; 1 st before and after each M every 1.5", 3 times. 161 (169, 177, 193, 209, 229, 249) sts.

Work from Body Flower chart over 35 rows, starting at st 1 (21, 17, 9, 1, 15, 5) and ending at st 65 (45, 49, 57, 65, 51, 61) from chart (repeat section between bold lines 6 (7, 7, 8, 8, 9, 10) times).

Next Row: With MC, P all sts.

Bottom Ribbing

Switch to smaller needles.
Work in K1, P1 Ribbing until band measures 1.5".
BO all sts in pattern.

Sleeves

Sleeves are worked in the round, from the top down. Sleeve caps are made from stitches picked up around armholes and are worked in short-rows.

Setup

With RS facing and beginning at center of underarm, PU and K 28 (29, 30, 31, 34, 36, 40) sts evenly spaced from base of armhole to shoulder "seam", PU and K 28 (29, 30, 31, 34, 36, 40) sts from shoulder "seam" to base of armhole. 56 (58, 60, 62, 68, 72, 80) sts.

Shape Cap

Setup short-row 1 (RS): K32 (33, 34, 35, 38, 40, 44) sts, W&T.
Setup short-row 2 (WS): P8 sts, W&T.
Short-row 1 (RS): K to last turning point, K wrapped st, K1, W&T.
Short-row 2 (WS): P to last turning point, P wrapped st, P1, W&T.
Rep last 2 rows 3 (3, 3, 4, 5, 6, 6) more times.
Short-row 3 (RS): K to last turning point, K wrapped st, W&T.
Short-row 4 (WS): P to last turning point, P wrapped st, W&T.
Rep last 2 rows 8 (9, 10, 9, 10, 10, 11) more times.
Short-row 5 (RS): K to last turning point, K wrapped st, K2, W&T.
Short-row 6 (WS): P to last turning point, P wrapped st, P2, W&T.
Rep last 2 rows 1 (1, 1, 1, 1, 1, 2) more times.
Next Row (RS): K to last turning point, K wrapped st, PM to denote underarm center. Do not turn. Start working in the round. Switch to DPNs or use the Magic Loop method.

Work even until sleeve measures 2" at underarm. Dec 1 st on each side of underarm M, then dec 1 st on each side of underarm M every 8 rnds 3 (2, 3, 3, 2, 2, 1) times, every 4 rnds 6 (8, 5, 6, 6, 7, 7) times, every 2 rnds 0 (0, 0, 0, 4, 2, 7) times (omit sets of instructions with 0 repetitions for your size). 36 (36, 42, 42, 42, 48, 48) sts.

Work even until sleeve measures 15.5 (15.75, 16, 16.25, 16.75, 17.25, 17.75)" from shoulder, or approximately 6.5" less than desired arm length.

Work from Sleeves Flower chart over 35 rows, starting at st 7 (7, 4, 4, 4, 1, 1) and ending at st 42 (42, 45, 45, 45, 48, 48) from chart.
Next Row: With MC, P all sts.

Wristband
Switch to smaller needles.
Work in K1, P1 Ribbing until band measures 1.5".
BO all sts in pattern.

Button Bands and Neckline
Left Button Band
With smaller needles, starting at top edge with RS facing, PU and K approximately 89 (89, 91, 91, 91, 93, 93) sts (or desired odd number of sts), picking up approximately 3 sts for every 4 rows. Work in K1, P1 Ribbing for 1". BO all sts in pattern.

Lay cardigan flat. Place a button aligned with the middle row of the bottom Fair Isle band, one button on the bottom ribbing band and measure space between the two. Place all buttons with this space between each of them. Mark buttons placement.

Buttonhole Band (right)
With smaller needles and RS facing, starting at bottom edge, PU and K approximately 89 (89, 91, 91, 91, 93, 93) sts (or same number as for left button band), picking up approximately 3 sts for every 4 rows. Work in K1, P1 Ribbing for 0.5". On the next row, *work in pattern to buttonhole placement, work buttonhole as K2tog, YO; rep from * through last buttonhole, work in pattern to end of row. Work in K1, P1 Ribbing for another 0.5". BO all sts in pattern.

Neckline
With smaller needles and RS facing, starting at top right edge, PU and K 42 (45, 46, 49, 50, 52, 55) sts from right front to shoulder "seam", 41 (43, 45, 49, 49, 53, 59) sts from back, 42 (45, 46, 49, 50, 52, 55) sts from left front. 125 (133, 137, 147, 149, 157, 169) sts. Work in K1, P1 Ribbing for 1", working a buttonhole above buttonhole band if desired. BO all sts in pattern.

Finishing
Weave in ends, wash and block to diagram.

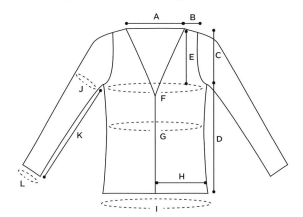

A 8.25 (8.5, 9, 9.75, 9.75, 10.5, 11.75)"
B 2.5 (2.5, 2.5, 2.5, 2.75, 2.75, 2.75)"
C 5.5 (5.75, 5.75, 6, 6.25, 6.25, 6.25)"
D 17 (17, 17.5, 17.5, 17.5, 17.75, 17.75)"
E 7 (7, 7, 7.75, 8, 8.25, 9)"
F 32.25 (33.75, 35.5, 38.5, 41.75, 45.75, 49.75)"
G 29.75 (31.5, 33, 36.25, 39.5, 43.5, 47.5)"
H 8 (8.5, 8.75, 9.5, 10.5, 11.5, 12.5)"
I 32.25 (33.75, 35.5, 38.5, 41.75, 45.75, 49.75)"
J 11.25 (11.5, 12, 12.5, 13.5, 14.5, 16)"
K 18 (18, 18, 18, 18, 18.25, 18.25)"
L 7.25 (7.25, 8.5, 8.5, 8.5, 9.5, 9.5)"

Sleeve Flower Chart

Legend

knit
RS: knit stitch
WS: purl stitch

MC
C1
C2
C3

pattern repeat

Body Flower Chart

FARA HAT AND MITTS

by Faye Kennington

 For pattern support, contact faye@coastandtoast.com

FINISHED MEASUREMENTS

Hat: 18 (20, 22, 24)" circumference, 11.5 (12, 12.5, 13)" high.

Mittens: 6 (7, 8, 9)" circumference, 9.25 (9.5, 9.5, 9.75)" long.

YARN

Knit Picks Bare Swish DK (100% Superwash Merino Wool; 246 yards/100g): MC Natural 24044, 1 ball.

Knit Picks Swish DK (100% Superwash Merino Wool; 123 yards/50g): C1 Garnet Heather 24315, 2 balls; C2 Honey 26061, 1 (2, 2, 2) balls.

NEEDLES

US 4 (3.5mm) DPNs and 16" circular needle, or one 32" or longer circular needle for Magic Loop technique, or size to obtain gauge

US 6 (4mm) DPNs and 16" circular needle, or one 32" or longer circular needle for Magic Loop technique, or size to obtain gauge

NOTIONS

Yarn Needle

Stitch Marker

Scrap Yarn

Pompom Maker (optional)

GAUGE

24 sts and 26 rows = 4" over stranded St st in the round on larger needles, blocked.

24 sts and 32 rows = 4" over St st in the round on smaller needles, blocked.

Fara Hat and Mitts

Notes:

This classic hat and mitts set is a breeze to work because most rows only use 2 colors of yarn at a time and there are no long floats.

Smaller needles are used in sections without stranded stitches, to match the finer gauge that often occurs with fair isle color work. At the end of every round, untwist the working yarn easily by holding each ball of yarn apart in the air and allowing the work to hang down and spin.

1x1 Ribbing (in the round over an even number of sts)
All Rnds: *K1, P1; rep from * to end.

Stockinette st (St st, worked flat/in the round over any number of sts):
Row 1 (RS): Knit.
Row 2 (WS): Purl.
To work flat, rep Rows 1-2. To work in the rnd, rep Row 1 every rnd.

Hat
DIRECTIONS

The hat is worked in the round from the brim to the crown. Unless using magic loop technique, begin with the circulars and switch to the DPNs when the number of sts becomes too small to comfortably work.

Brim

With smaller needles and C1, loosely CO 108 (120, 132, 144) sts and join in the rnd, being careful not to twist. PM for beginning of rnd.
Work 7 rnds of 1x1 Ribbing.
Knit 1 rnd.

Body

Change to larger needles. Work Gift Set chart around, repeating the chart row 18 (20, 22, 24) times across the rnd. After Gift Set chart is complete, change to smaller needles. With MC work in St st until hat measures 9.25 (9.5, 9.75, 10)".

Crown Decreases

Rnd 1: *K7 (8, 9, 10), K2tog; rep from * to end. 96 (108, 120, 132) sts.
Rnds 2, 3, 4: Knit.
Rnds 5: *K6 (7, 8, 9), K2tog; rep from * to end. 84 (96, 108, 120) sts.
Rnds 6, 7: Knit.
Rnd 8: *K5 (6, 7, 8), K2tog; rep from * to end - 72 (84, 96, 108) sts.
Rnds 9, 11, 13, 15, 17, 19, 21, 23: Knit.
Rnd 10: *K4 (5, 6, 7), K2tog; rep from * to end. 60 (72, 84, 96) sts.
Rnd 12: *K3 (4, 5, 6), K2tog; rep from * to end. 48 (60, 72, 84) sts.
Rnd 14: *K2 (3, 4, 5), K2tog; rep from * to end. 36 (48, 60, 72) sts.
Rnd 16: *K1 (2, 3, 4), K2tog; rep from * to end. 24 (36, 48, 60) sts.
18" size, skip to Rnd 23.
Rnd 18: *K - (1, 2, 3), K2tog; rep from * to end. - (24, 36, 48) sts.
20" size, skip to Rnd 23.
Rnd 20: *K - (-, 1, 2), K2tog; rep from * to end. - (-, 24, 36) sts.
22" size, skip to Rnd 23.

Rnd 22: *K - (-, -, 1), K2tog; rep from * to end. - (-, -, 24) sts.
Rnd 24, All Sizes: K2tog around. 12 sts.

Cut yarn, leaving a 6" tail. Thread tail through remaining 12 sts and pull firmly to close hole.

Finishing

Weave in ends, wash and block. With C2, make pompom and attach to top of hat.

Mittens (Make 2)
DIRECTIONS

The mittens are worked from cuff to fingers using DPNs or magic loop. The afterthought thumb is created by inserting temporary scrap yarn sts in the work, and then removing the scrap yarn and working a tube of knitting around the freed sts.

Cuff

With smaller needles and C1, loosely CO 36 (42, 48, 54) sts and join in the round, being careful not to twist. PM for beginning of rnd.
Work 2" of 1x1 Ribbing.
Knit 1 rnd.

Body

Change to larger needles. Work Gift Set chart Rnds 1-26, repeating the Gift Set chart row 6 (7, 8, 9) times across the rnd.
Rnd 27: Work 15 (18, 20, 23) sts according to Gift Set chart, K6 (6, 8, 8) sts with scrap yarn, Sl 6 (6, 8, 8) scrap sts back from RH needle to LH needle, work remaining 21 (24, 28, 31) sts as a continuation of chart Row 27.
Work remaining chart Rnds 28-32.

After Gift Set chart is complete, change to smaller DPNs. With MC work in St st until mitten measures 8.25 (8.5, 8.5, 8.75)".

Cuff

With C1, K 1 rnd.
Work 6 rows of 1x1 Ribbing.
BO loosely in pattern.

Thumb

Place needle through 1 leg of each of the 6 (6, 8, 8) sts above and below the scrap yarn sts. Remove the scrap yarn, PM and prepare to work in the round with C2.
Rnd 1: With RS facing, K6 (6, 8, 8) sts from needle below hole, PU 4 sts in side gap, K6 (6, 8, 8) sts from needle above hole, PU 4 sts in side gap. 20 (20, 24, 24) sts.
Rnd 2: *(K1, P1) 3 (3, 4, 4) times, K2tog, P2tog; rep from * twice. 16 (16, 20, 20) sts.
Work 6 rows of 1x1 Ribbing.
BO loosely in pattern.
Cut yarn, leaving a 6" tail.

Finishing

Use ends of thumb ribbing to sew up any holes on side gaps of thumb as necessary. Holes could also be closed by duplicate stitching over top as needed. Weave in ends, wash and block.

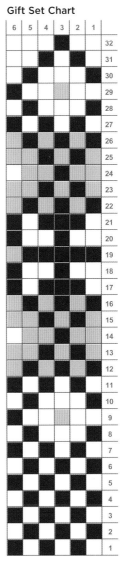

Gift Set Chart

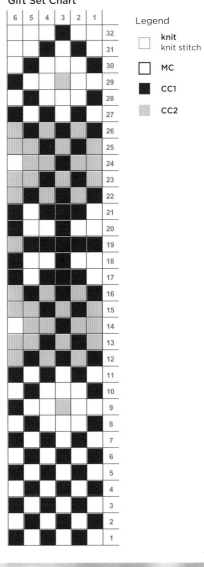

Legend

- ☐ **knit**
  knit stitch
- ☐ **MC**
- ■ **CC1**
- ▨ **CC2**

SILIA HAT

by Cristina Ghirlanda

FINISHED MEASUREMENTS

19.25" circumference
9.5" brim to center of crown

YARN

Knit Picks Palette (100% Peruvian
Highland Wool; 231 yards/50g): MC
Clarity 25548, C1 Marble Heather 24244,
C2 Asphalt Heather 24243; 1 ball each.

NEEDLES

US 2 (2.75mm) DPN's plus 16" circular
needle, or size to obtain gauge
US 1 (2.5mm) 16" circular needle, or one
size smaller than needle to obtain gauge,
for brim

NOTIONS

Yarn Needle
Stitch Markers

GAUGE

32.5 sts and 36 rows = 4" in stranded St
st (Snowflake Chart) in the round on larger
needle, blocked.

Silia Hat

Notes:

Read all charts from the right to the left. All empty square are knit stitches.

MC is the dominant color, hold that color to the left, independent of your knitting style.

You may wish to place markers at every pattern repeat to make it easier to follow the charts.

DIRECTIONS

With smaller needle and MC, use the Long-tail Method to loosely CO 136 sts.

Join and begin working in the round, being careful not to twist sts. PM at the beginning of round.

Round 1: *K2, P2; rep from * around.

Repeat Round 1 until piece measures 1".

Change to larger needle.

Next Round: (K5, KFB) 20 times, K to end of round. 156 sts.

Begin Charts

Work in Snowflake Chart around from Round 1 through Round 22 once.

Work in Pois Chart around from Round 1 through Round 6 a total of 5 times.

Crown Shaping

Work in Crown Shaping Chart around from Round 1 through Round 24 once. Change to DPN's when sts no longer fit comfortably on needle.

Finishing

Cut yarn and leave tail. Thread tail through the 13 live sts twice to secure.

Weave in ends, wash and block to measurements without stretching the ribbing.

Pois Chart

Crown Shaping Chart

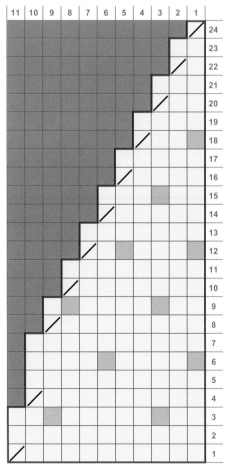

Snowflake Chart

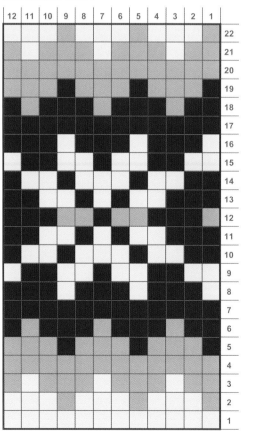

Legend

	knit
□	knit stitch
╱	**k2tog** — Knit two stitches together as one stitch
▨	**No Stitch** — Placeholder - No stitch made.
	MC
	C1
■	**C2**
—	**pattern repeat**

SUMMER WANES HAT AND COWL

by Heather Storta

FINISHED MEASUREMENTS

Cowl: 35" circumference x 13" high
Hat: 20.75" circumference at brim; 12"
height, 28" circumference at crown.

YARN

Knit Picks Palette (100% Peruvian Highland
Wool; 231 yards/50g): A White 23728, B
Cream 23730, C Coriander Heather 25544,
D Puma Heather 26059, E Briar Heather
26058, F Mongoose 25084, G Verdant
Heather 24006, H Forest Heather 24584, I
Autumn Heather 24002, J Brindle Heather
24004, K Turmeric 24251, L Semolina 24250;
1 ball each.

NEEDLES

US 1 (2.25mm) 16" circular needles, or size to
obtain gauge
US 2 (3mm) 16" for hat, 24" for cowl circular
needles, plus DPN's for hat, or size to obtain
gauge

NOTIONS

Yarn Needle
Stitch Markers

GAUGE

32 sts and 32 rows = 4" in stranded St st on
larger needles, blocked.
40 sts and 40 rows = 4" in Corrugated Rib
on smaller needles, blocked.

Summer Wanes Hat and Cowl

Notes:

This hat and cowl set was inspired by the autumn colors seen in the North Carolina mountains. The tam-style hat features corrugated ribbing at the brim and the same central panel used in the cowl. Read each chart row from right to left, as a RS row.

Corrugated Rib (in the round over an even number of sts)

Round 1: With color I, purl.
Round 2: With color I, knit.
Round 3: Join color A, *K1 with color I, K1 with color A; rep from * to end of rnd.
Round 4: *K1 with color J, P1 with color B; rep from * to end of rnd.
Round 5: Repeat Rnd 4.
Round 6: *K1 with color K, P1 with color C; rep from * to end of rnd.
Round 7: Repeat Rnd 6.
Round 8: *K1 with color L, P1 with color D; rep from * to end of rnd.
Round 9: Repeat Rnd 8.
Rounds 10, 11: Repeat Rnd 6.
Rounds 12, 13: Repeat Rnd 4.
Round 14: *K1 with color I, P1 with color A; rep from * to end of rnd.
Round 15: With color I, knit.
Round 16: With color I, purl.

Garter st (in the rnd over any number of sts)

Round 1: Purl.
Round 2: Knit.
Rep Rnds 1-2 for pattern.

Crown Decreases Chart

DIRECTIONS

Hat

Brim

Using color I and smaller needles, CO 208 sts. Join to work in the round, being careful not to twist sts. PM to indicate beginning of rnd.

Work Corrugated Rib pattern Rnds 1-16.

Inc Rnd: *K12, KFB; rep from * to end of rnd. 224 sts.

Body

Switch to larger needles. Begin working Summer Wanes chart. Work highlighted section (Rnds 21-75) of chart once, rep each chart row 4 times across the rnd.

Crown

Work Crown chart once, rep each chart row 8 times across the rnd. 32 sts.

Next Round: SM, K1, *K2tog; rep from * to last st in round, K2tog, removing marker. 16 sts.
Final Round: *K2tog 8 times around. 8 sts.

Cut yarn, leaving a long tail. Thread tail onto tapestry needle and run thread through remaining 8 sts. Tighten to neaten up hole.

Cowl

Using color I and larger needles, CO 280 sts. Join to work in the round, being careful not to twist sts. PM to indicate beginning of rnd.

Using color I, work in Garter st for 4 rows beginning with a purl row.

Begin working Summer Wanes chart, rep each chart row 5 times across the rnd. Work Rnds 1-94 of chart once.

Using color I, work in Garter st for 4 rows, beginning with a knit row.

BO all sts using color I.

Finishing

Weave in all ends, wash and block hat and cowl to diagrams.

Summer Wanes Chart

Legend

knit
knit stitch

No Stitch
Placeholder - No stitch made.

k2tog
Knit two stitches together as one stitch

ssk
Slip one stitch as if to knit, Slip another stitch as if to knit. Insert left-hand needle into front of these 2 stitches and knit them together

A

B

C

D

E

F

G

H

I

J

K

L

hat repeat